'Clear and equipping. This book h[...]
many churches to love God's childr[...]
trauma. It will aid understanding of [...]
people and their loved ones.'
Kara Ann Marie Smith, Orphan No More

'Writing as a theological tutor in an Anglican theological college, I am delighted to see the arrival of this book with its blend of education, Christian faith, psychotherapy and honesty.

'*Breakthrough: The Art of Surviving* is about how to survive with your faith and your inner world intact, because the author is so evidently a disciple of Christ. He notes, however, that prayer is not a shortcut to surviving abuse, but neither is psychology "of the devil". He shows current insight, detailing that lots of survivors connect with church, but many often struggle with church. More importantly, he offers open-ended and relevant conversation about the sexual orientation of survivors of sexual abuse, including referencing his own journey.'
Revd Dr Howard J Worsley, Vice Principal Trinity College, Bristol; Tutor in Missiology

'This is not an easy read, but it's a courageous, important read so that the church may understand abuse and the role it can play in supporting survivors. Well written it's as gentle as it is hard hitting whilst offering hope.'
Rachael Newham, author of Learning to Breathe

'This little book is a gem. It contains great wisdom, makes a lot of sense and is written by a survivor for survivors and their supporters. This is neither an academic book nor an autobiography, but a resource to make sense of the impact on us of abuse and to show us the direction of the path to recovery.

'This is a profoundly positive book and shows that there is more to trauma than meets the eye. The author understands abuse at a deep level and is writing from his lived experience of surviving, recovering and thriving. I have read a lot of books in this area, but this book connects with parts that other books don't reach!

'As a psychotherapist, the author has founded a charity to help survivors and train their supporters to provide hope and help while people heal. I so wish that mental health services would take the same positive view – that with the right help most people can recover from the negative impacts of childhood abuse, even the most terrible abuse that can be imagined or experienced.'

Dr Fergus Law MBChB, MSc, FRCPsych, Consultant Psychiatrist, and Senior Clinical Lecturer in Mental Health and Addiction at the University of Bristol

'It is way past time for the Church to engage with the depth of distress and angst surrounding the issue of abuse – abuse of children (and adults) through neglect and deliberate manipulation, and the use of children for the personal, sexual and emotional gratification of adults. Abuse is perpetrated in the Church as well as in the secular community – and we are equally culpable if we turn away because it offends our sensibilities, or challenges our abilities to cope with what we hear...

'Whether or not you agree with Giles' interpretation of these issues, he has undoubtedly earned the right to speak and to be heard. As a survivor of abuse and as a professional supporting individuals in their journeys towards healing, he offers insight, experience and skills for supporting those whom Jesus sought out – the marginalised, the shamed and the broken. I encourage you to read, to learn and to journey with him through this book, to lay aside prejudice and preconceived ideas, so that you might consider an alternative worldview, perhaps one that the Shepherd might present – that those who are lost need our understanding, our compassion, our energy, our patience and our perseverance. They are already doing the best they can – can we meet them in their pain and draw on our additional reserves to support and comfort them as they heal?

'This is a much-needed commentary on these issues; there is room for more, but this is a door opened. I hope you will summon your courage and engage with this first offering.'
Lindsay Schofield, BABCP Accred, MBACP Accred, MNCP Snr Accred, ACC Accred, MNCS Prof Accred/Supervision, Psychotherapist and Supervisor from Cornerstone Integrated Therapy

BREAKTHROUGH
THE ART OF SURVIVING

Giles D. Lascelle

instant
apostle

First published in Great Britain in 2019

Instant Apostle
The Barn
1 Watford House Lane
Watford
Herts
WD17 1BJ

Every effort has been made to seek permission to use copyright material reproduced in this book. The publisher apologises for those cases where permission might not have been sought and, if notified, will formally seek permission at the earliest opportunity.

The views and opinions expressed in this work are those of the author and do not necessarily reflect the views and opinions of the publisher.

British Library Cataloguing-in-Publication Data

A catalogue record for this book is available from the British Library.

This book and all other Instant Apostle books are available from Instant Apostle:

Website: www.instantapostle.com

E-mail: info@instantapostle.com

ISBN 978-1-912726-14-1

Printed in Great Britain.

For God has not given us a spirit of fear, but of power and of love and of a sound mind.

2 Timothy 1:7 (NKJV)

Acknowledgements

Although the author gets all the attention, writing a book and bringing it to the readers really is a team effort. I have been incredibly blessed to have had the support of a number of amazing people, without whom this book would never have seen the light of day.

First and foremost I have to thank my wife Ally, who has selflessly put up with being a writing widow for the last year. I really could not have done this without your love, encouragement and your willingness to release me to write during evenings and weekends. Thank you for all that you have given up, so this book could reach the people who need it. You have always been my number one fan, and you mean the world to me.

I also want to thank the wonderful people at Instant Apostle who have supported this book ever since they first heard about it, and have put their resources and skills behind it in every possible way – from copy-editing to the great cover art, marketing, etc.

I would like to acknowledge all those who have supported the project financially and in other ways, and who by their generosity have helped to bring the book to print. You have asked to remain anonymous, but you know who you are and I am deeply grateful to you all.

I must also acknowledge the immense debt of gratitude I owe to all the survivors I have had the privilege of working with over the last thirty years. Your courage, your stories of hope and your resilience in following this journey of recovery and healing have inspired me in ways I can only begin to describe.

Last but not least, I want to give a huge thank you to the team at Breakthrough – staff, volunteers and trustees. I can only do what I do because you are right there supporting me and those we work with. Thank you for all that you do. In particular I want to thank our media and development person – I know you don't want to be named, but I want to honour the incredible time and effort you have put in to promoting both the book and the charity. You challenged me to start writing, and continued to show your excitement about the project by very lovingly bullying and encouraging me to keep going. I know that without your 'tough love' this book would probably never have been finished.

Contents

Contents

Introduction

Who is this book by?

When I started writing this book, the very first question I asked myself was not the usual *Who is this book aimed at?* but *Who is this book by?* Not because I'm having some sort of identity crisis, but more because there are a number of different perspectives from which I could be thought of as qualified to write a book about surviving childhood abuse. The more I wrote the more I realised that those different perspectives all support and inform one another.

A survivor
First and foremost, I am writing from the perspective of being a survivor of childhood abuse. My own story and who I am as a person are shaped by having been severely abused throughout my childhood, from pre-school to late teens, both by people within my immediate family and outside. However, although I do refer to these events, in particular where they will help illustrate a point, this is not essentially an autobiographical work.

Nevertheless, I realise that writing from the perspective of being a survivor allows me to share things from my own lived experience, rather than mere theoretical knowledge. If we think about it, the people who know most about how to survive and how to reclaim our lives following childhood abuse are those of us who have suffered and survived. That should probably be obvious, but unfortunately it is something that all too often gets missed by the professionals who work with survivors. When all is said and done, anyone who has reached adulthood after a history of being abused as a child has already come through many hard battles, and has already proved themselves to be victorious.

To be fair to the professionals, though, many of us who have survived abusive childhoods also lose sight at times of the fact that we are survivors. We don't see ourselves as victorious, or overcomers, or any of that stuff. All we see and feel is the pain, distress and difficulty. This isn't because we are weak or stupid. It is because the very things that helped us to survive when we were little are now the things that cause us to struggle in adult life. As a result, we tend to discount our victories, and believe that we are getting it wrong.

As a survivor, my heart has always been to be a support and a resource to other survivors. Therefore, a large part of my purpose in writing this book is to remind and encourage us (I include myself here) that even if we have forgotten, even if we never fully realised it, we had and still have what it takes to survive and break through to a full and abundant life.

A psychotherapist

I am also writing this book from the point of view of a psychotherapist and a professional helper. It is probably fair to say that I never planned to do the work I do. I seemed to drift into it by accident. However, for the last thirty years I have found myself working with some of the most broken and abused people – firstly in Social Services, with young offenders and children in care, during which time I trained as a psychotherapist. After that I worked with dependent drug users, then with NHS staff and in private practice, and discovered that the majority of my clients had experienced abuse as children. Currently, I work for a Christian charity that I founded, which works with adult survivors of childhood abuse and trauma.

There is a sense in which my experience as a survivor cannot fully be separated from my career as a therapist. Each informs the other one. What my experience as a therapist has given me is a way to give shape to and make sense of my experience as a survivor. This in turn helps me to understand some of the ways in which trauma, and in particular child abuse, impacts the human soul, mind and body. It has also helped me to develop ways in which not only can therapists help survivors, but in which therapists can also equip survivors to help themselves.

An educator

Almost as important is the sense in which I am writing this book from the perspective of an educator and trainer. A large part of my professional life has involved running training courses for a whole range of people, most often in what are called the helping professions. Much of that role as a trainer involves equipping people – giving them skills, teaching them how to do things and so on. But another of the functions of a trainer is to be an educator – someone who offers a different perspective and helps people to think about things in new and creative ways.

My present focus is very much on educating people in the Christian world (church leaders, ministry leaders, prayer teams and so on) about the impact of child abuse on adults, and how best to help and support them. However, the Christian world is in many ways something of a microcosm of the wider society, so this book is also written from the perspective of someone who is passionate about getting the message out there that we have to do better when it comes to understanding the needs of survivors, and how to help them recover, heal and reclaim their lives.

A disciple

Last, but by no means least, I am writing this book as a disciple – meaning one who follows. As one who for the last twenty years has been learning to love and follow Jesus Christ, I am aware just how much my deepening relationship with Him has affected me both personally and professionally.

At a personal level, as a survivor, I know that without Him as a model of wholeness and integration, I would not have been able to heal to the extent that I have. I know that without His unlimited and unconditional goodness and love holding me, I would long ago have fallen into an endless black hole. I know that without the light that He is, I would long ago have been swallowed up by the darkness.

As a psychotherapist (literally a soul healer) I have to rely on Christ's leading to guide me through what is often a rugged and dangerous landscape, as I walk with people on their journey of recovery and healing. I also know that to the extent that we will let Him, He sustains and embraces every single survivor in ways that are often mysterious and unfathomable, but which always demonstrate His great heart and love for those who are broken, marginalised and in darkness.

Who is this book for?

Sometimes as authors we are told to imagine our target audience as a person – a single ideal reader – and imagine that we are writing solely for them. In this book I have to imagine three people – three ideal readers, if you like.

Survivors of abuse

Firstly and most importantly, this book is written for adult survivors of childhood abuse. All of us who share this experience know what a hard journey it can be to recover and heal from the effects of what happened to us. Sometimes as we make our way through the world we really can feel like 'a stranger in a strange land' (Exodus 2:22, KJV). Things that other people take for granted can seem very problematic and different for us. All in all, for survivors, the world, along with life and everything that goes with it, can feel like a very unfamiliar, challenging and even hostile place.

This book attempts to be something of a guidebook, with resources to help us on our journey of healing and recovery. Some of it will apply to all of us – there are certain things that are common to all survivors of abuse – and other parts will apply only to some of us. But whatever the type of abuse we experienced, there should be something in here for all of us.

Supporters and helpers

Secondly, my intention is that this book will be of help to those who are supporting and helping survivors of childhood abuse. By this I do not necessarily mean professional helpers. Of course they have a role too, but really what I mean is our friends, our (non-abusive) family and other loved ones. The truth is that no one can make this journey of recovery on their own. Although it is sometimes hard for survivors to admit it, we need people around us who love and care about us. But it also helps if those people have some understanding of what has happened to us, what we are going through now, and why we respond to things in some of the ways we do.

This book, then, is also intended as a resource and a guidebook for those who are accompanying survivors on their journey of healing and recovery. If you are one of those supporters, thank you. I hope this book will give you some insight and some ideas for how to be there for those you love and care about. We know you are very willing, and you really want to help. However, we also know, even if we don't often say it, that this can be a rough journey for you as well. You want to support and do whatever you can to make our lives easier, but there are times when that can feel quite overwhelming and even intimidating. There are times when we have some pretty strong reactions to things, and you don't even know what it is that has set us off. Half the time neither do we, or if we do, we don't necessarily know how to explain it to you. So this journey that you have so wonderfully agreed to accompany us on is going to take a lot of patience and understanding from you at times. Hopefully this book can help you understand, and with understanding may come the patience and the energy you need to continue walking with us, as we journey towards recovery and healing.

Christian leaders

Lastly, this book is also intended to be helpful to Christian leaders. By leaders, I mean in the broadest possible sense to include not only ministers and leaders of churches, but also small group leaders, people on ministry teams, prayer teams and so on. One of the things I have discovered as I have run training sessions in various church settings is that church leaders and those who serve on ministry teams often have a great heart for the broken and marginalised, including those who have survived childhood abuse. However, they don't necessarily always have the information and understanding necessary to help in the ways that they might like. This has sometimes led to some tensions between churches and their leadership on the one hand, and survivors and their supporters on the other.

Hopefully this book will be a resource for leaders and those who serve on ministry teams, who desire to do something different. My aim is that it will enable them to see where there may have been misunderstandings and difficulties in the past, and how they may be able to move forward in offering survivors of childhood abuse the support and care that they need and deserve.

How to use this book

This book is intended to be a companion; something we can take with us on our journey of recovery and healing. I have tried to structure it in a reasonably logical way, so that those who wish to can read it through from beginning to end and see a progression in how we understand, think about and respond to the trauma of child abuse. However, some people may prefer to dip in and out of particular chapters and sections that seem relevant to whatever challenges they are currently facing.

At the end of some chapters you will find a section entitled *Survivor Resources*. These are practical ideas, exercises and other resources that can help survivors on their journey of recovery and healing. They are primarily aimed at survivors themselves, though they will also be of interest for those who support survivors. They are written for the most part in the first person – in other words, using what is called 'I Language'. The reason for this is that very often those who were traumatised as children have had a large part of their thinking and their belief systems defined, manipulated and controlled by others – usually by the people who abused them or who enabled the abuse to take place. One of the most subtle forms of damage caused by child abuse is that very often this 'victim' thinking becomes internalised, and the survivor takes on a view of themselves and their world that is essentially mirroring the perspectives and beliefs of their abusers.

By writing these resources in the first person, the intention is that as they are used by survivors, that process can gradually be reversed. By speaking them out, or reading them in the first person, survivors are engaging with the language of their own internal narratives and dialogues. In this way they are empowered to bring change to the typical perspectives and beliefs that characterise the victims of childhood abuse. Over time their self-talk can shift towards narratives that are more orientated to survival, and to breaking through the limitations imposed by their abusers.

Some chapters also have what I've called *Supporter's Pause for Thought*. These are simply one or two thoughts or questions designed to be a gentle prompt to those who are supporting survivors, whether friends and loved ones or leaders in church settings. They can be used to provoke thinking, either individually or in small group settings.

In short, these resources aim to enable survivors to live lives that are more real, full and healthy.

Note on examples used

I have used a number of stories and examples in this book to illustrate various points. Even where particular survivors gave permission for their stories to be used, names and key details have been changed so that the people involved cannot be identified. For other examples I have drawn from a number of different people and situations to create what are essentially fictional accounts of experiences typical of survivors of abuse.

Chapter One
You Are a Survivor

This is for you

There is something I want to say right at the beginning of this book, and it is particularly for those of you who were abused as children. In fact, it's something that every one of us who was abused as a child needs to hear and be reminded of on a regular basis.

It is simply this. Even though we were victimised, we do not have to remain as victims. Abuse taught us to think of ourselves as victims, because we were made to feel powerless, not in control of our bodies, our minds and our lives. But the truth is we are survivors. Every single person reading this who experienced abuse as a child is a survivor. We've survived! We've made it this far, despite everything our abusers did to us. We are here! We may be bruised and battered in body, mind or spirit, but we are alive, and they have not managed to crush out the spark of life from us.

There are times, maybe many times, when we feel defeated and beaten down by life, but the reality is that we are not on the losing side. We are winners. Every day that we manage to keep on going, keep on living our lives despite everything that has happened, despite everything we feel, is a victory. It is a battle won against those who sought to destroy us. These may seem like small victories, but in fact they are huge. We are in a war. It wasn't one of our choosing. We were invaded and subjugated against our will, but we have chosen to go on living. We have chosen to go on surviving. This is a war of survival and hope, and like all wars it will not be won by a single spectacular victory. It will be won by hundreds, even thousands, of small daily acts of resistance that build slowly one upon another, until they gain a momentum that becomes unstoppable.

Breakthrough is possible

This is the other thing we need to remember: breakthrough is possible.

One of the things that characterises our lives as survivors is the sense we all have at times that we are not getting anywhere fast. We make progress, only to get knocked back again. We think we're moving forward, only to realise that we've been going round and round in circles. We try to get help, only to find that we've gone down a dead end.

There are practical reasons for this sense, of course. Life as a survivor is often not very straightforward. However, it is also in part due to the fact that our expectations were set by the abuse we experienced. When we were children there was no way out for us, or at least if there was, we didn't know how to get to it. We felt trapped and hemmed in, and that feeling persists in us right up to adulthood. But the basis of that feeling, just as with our sense of victimhood, is not actually true. Breakthrough is possible, and more than possible. The fact that we have survived means that we are stronger and far more resourceful than we think. Even if the external means for creating a breakthrough in our lives does not seem to be present, we have abundant internal resources. We have inner strength far beyond the obvious. What we do not have, at least until we learn how, is a means to access those resources.

This book is all about giving survivors the means to access the internal strength and resources they have forgotten they possess. It is these resources that will make breakthrough possible for us.

If breakthrough is possible, what is it we are breaking through to?

It's a fair question. We talk a great deal about the journey of healing and recovery from abuse, but sometimes we don't have a clear idea of where that journey might be leading us. Many survivors seem to feel that all they can reasonably expect is a life that is OK-ish. We believe that the wounds we carry and the emotional baggage mean we have to settle for a sort of second-class life – a life in which we make do with the bare minimum of the things that make life worth living. We look at the rest of the world through envious lenses, believing that the life that is available to us can never match up to the one available to others, because when it comes right down to it, we believe that *we* can never really match up. Our sense of self and our estimation of our own value have been so diminished by what has happened to us that our expectations are catastrophically lowered. We feel like second-class citizens of a world that really would rather not be aware that we and our issues exist. For those of us who have a faith, we may even feel as if we are second-class children of God. If we are going to change those feelings, we need to know that more is possible.

The good news is that this is not all there is. The journey goes on a long way beyond OK. Jesus was clear that He had come so that we (by which He means all of us) could have life 'in abundance' (John 10:10, Amplified Version). *Abundance* is an interesting word. It's sometimes translated as 'fullness', but that doesn't really do it justice. Abundance has connotations of being more than full, of being overflowing. So from the perspective of Jesus, everything He did and continues to do is so that we can have a life that overflows with goodness.

For most survivors that may seem a little too good to be true – more of a pious hope than an everyday lived reality. We want to believe it's possible, but deep down we suspect we may end up disappointed once again. The problem is, we are living our lives. We are faced with the evidence of our wounds every day, and we know what it feels like to keep tripping over them. We wince as yet another relationship runs into difficulty. We feel shame at our seeming inability to deal with the normal ups and downs of life in the way others seem to find so easy. We find ourselves wrestling with anxiety or falling into a black hole of depression with monotonous regularity. Surely this life overflowing with goodness has to be just one more thing that is out of reach? All of these experiences are true, and deeply painful, which makes it all the more important that we find ways of holding on to hope in the face of evidence that things are hopeless.

One of the ways we can do this is by understanding the nature of our breakthrough.

A journey of empowerment

Sometimes my psychotherapy clients tease me about how often I talk about their *journey*. The reason is that it is such a good metaphor for the process of healing and recovery from trauma. It is also a very necessary one. Journeys have a beginning, a middle and an end. They can be long or short, and they may go through many different types of landscape or terrain. While we are on that journey, we may find all sorts of obstacles that we need to overcome, but also many different things to discover and learn. Every journey has its destination, but the destination is never going to be the whole experience.

When we look at the lives of those around us, and in particular the lives of those who have not experienced the abuse and trauma we have, we can be tempted to feel that they have 'arrived', that they have reached their destination. We focus on the destination and, although we long for it, we fear it may be out of our reach. Of course it is! We are still on the journey.

The destination – the life overflowing with goodness – is something we have to keep in mind. We have to keep hoping or we have little or no incentive to keep on going through all the tough times. But abundance, wholeness and freedom are not the fruit of a single moment. They are things we grow into through our journeying and wandering in the wilderness. There is a reason why the Bible is so full of stories about journeys. Whether it is the children of Israel in the exodus from Egypt, the journey of encounter that Jesus took into the wilderness, or the journey of the prodigal son, they all have one thing in common – those who are on these journeys are shaped by them.

When the children of Israel left the slavery of Egypt, they were free in body. The journey across the desert to the promised land of abundance should have taken them two to three days, but they were not ready for their destination. Their minds and spirits still followed the same patterns of thinking, feeling and reacting, as if they were still in bondage. As well as seeing it as a historical account of God's dealings with Israel, it may also be helpful at the same time to read the story as something of a parable about how each one of us makes our journey out of bondage to freedom and abundance.

As survivors we have a journey to make from the slavery of being a victim of abuse into the 'promised land' of freedom and an abundant life. In practice that journey of recovery and growth is far from straightforward or quick.

We may be free of the abuse we suffered, at least in as much as we are no longer under the direct control of our abusers. Nevertheless, we still have the mindsets, the attitudes of heart and the responses of those who are still enslaved by abuse. We need a breakthrough, and we need to be set free, but we don't break through to our destination; we break through to our journey. Of course, the quick-fix solutions, the instant cures and the golden calves are always going to appeal to us. Every single creature is wired to avoid pain and discomfort. When we have already been through so much, why wouldn't we hanker after a shortcut to the destination?

One of the hardest things for us to learn as survivors is that there are no shortcuts. If there were, the destination would be different. Contrary to what we may want to believe, it is the journey cut short that leads to the second-class life. When we are tempted to cheat ourselves of the journey, the wholeness and freedom we discover at the end of it is superficial. It looks good on the outside, but inside we are still suffering the pain and distress of wounds that have not adequately healed or been cleansed of infection.

The truth is, we are survivors, not because we have come to the end of our journey, or even because we have reached a certain point along the way. We are survivors because we have chosen to begin. We have chosen to embrace the journey of healing and recovery, wherever it may lead us, in full knowledge that it will be hard and painful at times, but still holding on to hope, and open to the possibility of being transformed by the discoveries we make along the way.

Survivor Resources: Ten things to remind myself each day

Sometimes my thoughts and feelings can seem overwhelming, and it is really hard to find the positives in my life. I try to remind myself of these ten things every day – especially the headings in bold. If any of them strike a particular chord, or if I find some of them particularly challenging, I can read through the paragraph attached to it and think about how it might relate to me and my life.

1. Struggling is nothing to be ashamed of.

It is normal for me to struggle. The abuse I experienced was not normal or OK, and it has left me carrying emotional injuries that make life challenging sometimes. This is nothing for me to be ashamed of, any more than someone with an injured leg needs to be ashamed for limping. I struggle, but I keep on going. Every day that I get up out of bed, every time I manage to do the things I need to do, is a win. I may be struggling, but struggling means I haven't given up. I am a survivor.

2. Expressing emotions is OK.

When I was little I wasn't allowed to express the fear, pain, anger and sadness I felt about being abused. But those emotions didn't go away. They stayed locked up inside me, and I've been carrying them around with me for years. Life is challenging enough without me having to carry the weight of all these feelings. Expressing my emotions doesn't make me bad, or mean that I'm not OK. It means that I value myself enough to let out all that pain rather than letting it continue to poison my life. It's time for me to learn how to let my feelings out, so I can move on with my life.

3. I have the resources I need to survive and thrive.

Sometimes I feel that I cannot cope. I feel that the pain of the abuse I suffered is going to break me, and I just don't have what it takes to become whole again. But I know this isn't true. The truth is, I found ways to survive back then when I was being abused. Even though I was only a child, and didn't have the power to stop what was happening, I still found the inner resources to make it through. Just as I found the resources then, I can find the resources now. Who I was as a person was enough then, and it is enough now. The only difference is that now I can find resources outside myself to help me on my journey of recovery and healing.

4. I don't need to compare myself with others.

It is so easy to compare myself with others, but it's really not helpful. The truth is, no one can fully know about another's journey. When I look at others and think they are doing so much better than I am, I'm not seeing them in their hardest moments. When I'm worried that others are looking at me and judging me for my lack of progress, the chances are they're not, and even if they are, they don't know all the complexities and challenges I face every day. I am me, and I am walking this journey the best way I know how.

5. I am strong enough to make good choices.

It isn't always easy for me to make good choices about my life. For a long time, coping has sometimes meant that I make the choices that help me to feel better in the short term, rather than the ones that are most helpful in the long run. But I am strong, and I'm growing stronger every day I walk this path of recovery and healing. One choice at a time, I am learning to do the things that move me closer to a life that is healthy, happy and filled with love.

6. It's OK to make mistakes.

I don't need to be perfect, and I don't need to give myself a hard time when I make mistakes. Who I am and how I am is good enough. Mistakes are evidence that I keep on going and keep on trying to live my life free from the effects of the abuse. When I try, and things still go wrong, it marks a place where life got tough and I needed a bit more practice or a bit more help to keep moving forward. When things go wrong, I stop and I take responsibility for any impact it may have had on another person. Then I give myself credit for trying, even though it didn't go quite right, and consider what I can do differently next time.

7. Being kind to myself costs nothing.

When I was little I was supposed to get kindness and love and care. But what I got instead was abuse and neglect and punishment. Sometimes even now I find it hard to give myself anything other than more abuse, neglect and punishment. But I deserved better when I was little, and I deserve better now. Being kind to myself costs nothing. In fact, it is a way of investing in myself and my life. If I invest just a little kindness – love, care and nurture – in myself, it is like planting seeds and watering them daily. Eventually they will grow, and the love and kindness I have invested will flourish and bear fruit.

8. Asking for help is strength not weakness.

There is nothing strong about trying to do everything all by myself and falling flat on my face. When people offer to help me stay standing or keep moving forward, there is nothing strong about pushing them and their help away. That type of strength is actually just pride. When I am physically injured, it's not weak if I go and get help to patch myself up. It is the same when I am injured in my mind and emotions. There is nothing wrong with realising I can't do it all by myself, and I'm willing to put aside my pride to ask people to give me the help I need. When I ask for help I am learning what it really means to be strong.

9. I am worthy of care and love.
When they abused me and neglected me and failed to meet my needs when I was a child, they tried to make me believe that I was unworthy. They tried to make me believe I didn't get what I needed because I didn't deserve it. The truth is I am worthy. My worthiness doesn't rest in what I do, what I achieve, what I look like, what I have, what I do for a living or how many friends I have. It doesn't even depend on me getting things right. I am worthy because of who I am. I am worthy because every human being is worthy of care, love and belonging. Even though I don't always feel like I fit in or that I'm like other people, there are no exceptions. I am worthy because I am worthy.

10. This will get better!
No matter how bad I feel right now, it isn't going to stay like this. When I feel scared, or sad, or ashamed, or hopeless, I can't always see an end to it, but there always is an end if I am willing to stick with it for long enough. These are the times I need to remember how things were in the past. I need to remember the other times when I thought it was going to be like this forever. I always came out of it eventually. It may have taken time, and maybe I only came out for a little while, but it did change, and that means this too will change. This is a moment to dig deep and hold on tight, because no matter how hopeless it feels, and no matter how dark it seems, there is hope and there is light just over the horizon.

Supporter's Pause for Thought: What can I give?

Our love and compassion are not measured in feelings; they are measured in what and how we can give to those who may not at this point be able to give anything in return. When you think about the one you are supporting, ask yourself *how can I best show this person my love and care for them*? It could be a kind word, a small gift, a selfless act of service, time to listen or, with permission, a gentle touch.

Think, if necessary ask, and then do.

Chapter Two
Abuse and What it Does to Us

Abuse isn't glamorous

It is 1991. A couple of decades before Rotherham and the grooming gang scandals come to light. I am working for Social Services in a residential project for what we call 'emotionally and behaviourally disturbed young people'. They are aged fourteen and upward, and are supposedly being prepared for life outside the care system. I am working the overnight sleep-in shift, and around 1.30 am I hear a noise from one of the kids' rooms, the sound of adult voices laughing. I go down the passageway to investigate. I can hear a number of adult males talking inside one of the girl's rooms. I open the door and go in. There is a man in his forties having sex with one of the female residents, aged fifteen, while six other men look on, passing comment. One of the men appears to be videoing the proceedings. There is a frantic scramble as the men barge their way out of the room and down the stairs to get out of the building, leaving the girl in tears.

Later, once she is dressed, as we wait for the police to arrive, we talk. She tells me it has been going on for months, and that a number of the residents are involved. The men are all taxi drivers, and they give the girls alcohol, drugs and sometimes money to have sex with them.

'It's OK,' she says. 'It's no worse than my dad and my uncles used to do. At least I get something out of this.' The tears on her face give the lie to her matter-of-fact tone of voice.

When the police search her room later, they find three wraps of heroin. It turns out she's been smoking it for most of the six months she's been in the unit.

'It helps afterwards,' she says. 'It stops me feeling like such a total slag.'

Child abuse, and the trauma that results from it, is not glamorous or pretty. It doesn't get a lot of love in terms of public perception. Generally speaking, it comes some way down the priority list when it comes to charitable giving. When public attention is directed towards childhood abuse, we tend to think in terms of the children who have been victims. This is right and understandable; however, what sometimes seems to be forgotten is that the legacy of childhood abuse can last a lifetime. *Adult* survivors of abuse (the people this book is for and about) more or less drop off the public radar altogether. There seems to be very little in the way of understanding that the pain and distress of child abuse carries on, often for decades, in the form of post-traumatic stress. The whole subject is surrounded by myths, distortions and misunderstandings.

In recent years post-traumatic stress has in fact arrived on the public radar, but most people have no idea that the most common source of post-traumatic stress is actually abuse and maltreatment in childhood. If they think about it at all, the likelihood is that they think in terms of combat veterans or refugees. The stark reality is that everyone's life is affected both by childhood abuse and by the *legacy* of childhood abuse that endures and continues to impact life long after the original traumatic experiences have ended.

Whether you have experienced child abuse yourself, or whether you are a family member, a friend or a supporter of someone who has experienced abuse, or even if you don't think you know anyone who has experienced abuse – your life has still been impacted by it in ways you do not yet understand. There are of course plenty of hard facts and figures, but I don't want to overwhelm you. So I'm just going to give you the bottom line.

One in five of us in the UK (and the figures are pretty similar in most developed nations) has experienced significant abuse, maltreatment or other severe trauma as a child.[1] Just pause for a moment to let that sink in and consider the implications. One-fifth of the people you see walking the streets, in your workplace, in your circle of friends and family, has experienced some form of significant abuse or other trauma as a child or young person. One-fifth. That means quite literally millions of people, just in this country.

The other thing to understand is that childhood abuse and the trauma associated with it isn't like a bad dose of the flu. It isn't something that happens to a lot of us, and sadly a few people succumb to the effects and have further complications. It isn't something the vast majority of us recover from relatively quickly with nothing much in the way of long-lasting effects. Abuse in childhood is nothing

---

[1] L Radford, et al, 'Child Abuse and Neglect in the UK Today' (London: NSPCC, 2011).

38

like that. The effects go on and on and on, continuing to adversely affect us, often throughout our entire lives.

In this chapter, we are going to take a look at just what exactly we mean by childhood abuse, and we're going to do a quick overview of some of the main ways in which abuse continues to have a negative impact on those of us who have survived such abuse throughout our adult lives. In subsequent chapters we are going to go into the impact in a fair bit more detail. But we are also going to look at the positive side – how people can survive trauma, recover and break through into a life of wholeness and fulfilment.

What do we mean by trauma?

In order to understand the impact of the abuse we experienced as children, we need to understand trauma. Trauma is a slightly slippery concept, in that it means different things to different people. If you talk to a medical doctor, trauma most often refers to a physical injury such as a bruise or a wound. But when we think about the trauma we experienced as survivors of abuse, we are referring primarily to emotional or psychological trauma. Of course, sometimes the two are linked. A physical injury can very often lead to a psychological injury. The mind (not to be confused with the physical brain), by which we mean the patterns of thinking, feeling, perceiving and relating that make us who we are, becomes injured and damaged by what has happened to us. Therefore, our working definition of psychological trauma – what we are referring to simply as *trauma* – is this: an event or events that are so shocking that they cause an enduring negative impact to our ways of thinking, feeling, perceiving and relating – with regard to ourselves, others and the world around us.

In many ways the concept of *injury* is a very helpful way to think about trauma. Despite the tendency of the mental health professions to see everything in terms of what is called *the disease model*, trauma is not a disease or an illness any more than a physical wound is a disease or an illness. It is, however, something that can have a lasting effect on us, and it is something that we may well need help to heal and recover from.

Trauma can come from many different sources, and it is worth remembering that most trauma is not the result of deliberate malice or wrongdoing. Much trauma can come about as a result of accidental occurrences or the incidental ups and downs of life. Anyone who has ever been in or even witnessed a bad car accident, for example, will know that it can be very traumatising and can have some long-lasting effects. However, in the normal run of events, the emotional impact of that trauma will get better over time. This is what is sometimes known as *simple* trauma – though of course it can still be highly distressing for those who experience it. Some trauma may be caused by incidental factors – for example, the child who because of a difficult birth has to spend the first few days or weeks of life in an incubator rather than with its mother, or the child whose mother has to be absent from them due to illness. This too can lead to ongoing distress, but again, with the right sort of ongoing care and love from close family or other caregivers, many of those effects can be mitigated to a certain degree.

However, as we know only too well, the most damaging forms of trauma are neither accidental nor incidental. Rather they are the result of deliberate maltreatment and abuse, most particularly in childhood. We are going to be talking a fair bit about the ways in which this is so damaging, and the reasons for that, as we go along. However, to try to put it in a nutshell, there is something about deliberate maltreatment and abuse that is incredibly invasive, and in particular it does enormous damage to the way we see ourselves. Trauma as a result of accidental or incidental events can be explained as random occurrences or just part of life. Being a victim of child abuse makes us feel as if we are a target, and even that there is something about who we are that has made us a target for such horrible treatment. Because of this, the trauma experienced by those of us who have been victims of child abuse is far more complex and damaging than the vast majority of trauma that arises from accidental or incidental events.

Pinning down abuse

I also want to be really clear about what constitutes childhood abuse. This is particularly important because those who perpetrate abuse on children are particularly adept at trying to wriggle out of any responsibility for what they've done. Many of them even lie to themselves, trying to convince their victims and themselves that what they are doing isn't actually abuse. They call it by different names to make it sound palatable, acceptable and even virtuous. As a result, survivors of abuse tend to internalise those views about what has happened to them, and they minimise the impact it has had. In fact, in many cases, those of us who have been abused as children don't always fully realise that what happened to us was abuse. We need to pin down our definition, to ensure that the truth is the winner, and not the lies of those who perpetrate abuse on others.

One of first things that all survivors have to face on their journey of healing is that recovery from the trauma of child abuse begins when we are able to acknowledge to ourselves and to others that what happened to us was not normal or acceptable, but was in fact abusive and damaging.

So these are the things we mean by child abuse…

Neglect

Children have certain basic physical and emotional needs. The physical needs are fairly obvious. They need to be well fed, to be warm, to be clothed, to be clean and to have their health needs attended to. If any of these things are consistently absent, the child will not be healthy and thrive. But children also have some basic emotional needs. They need to be loved, to be comforted, to feel valued and to feel secure and protected. If any of these emotional needs are neglected, then the child will not develop a healthy sense of who they are, and this in turn is likely to have a long-term impact on their mental and physical health. In my working life helping survivors of trauma, I encounter many people who were not looked after physically as children. They were not adequately fed or clothed. They were not changed or bathed regularly enough. They were not talked to or played with or given the attention they needed. I also encounter many who were perfectly well looked after as children, at least in a physical sense. However, their families were deserts of love, affirmation and affection. They weren't hugged, or held, or made to feel that they had value.

Emotional abuse

Emotional abuse is a bit of a catch-all term. It covers forms of deliberate maltreatment that do not have a physical component. As such it might include some forms of emotional neglect, as mentioned above, but it could also cover things like verbal abuse, bullying, humiliation, hurtful criticism, name-calling, manipulation, etc. Just to be clear, we are not talking about the things children sometimes do to each other, but rather we are talking about things that adults are doing to children.

Sometimes emotional abuse can be very subtle and insidious. It may, for example, include a parent who refuses to talk with or respond to a child. It could include humiliating a child as a form of punishment. It could include such things as manipulating or persuading a child to do things they're not comfortable with, or making a child feel responsible for the consequences of adult actions. It could include expecting a child to take more responsibility for things than is appropriate to their age.

One of the most subtle things about emotional abuse is that very often there are no physical signs that a child is being maltreated. Dr Susan Forward in her book *Toxic Parents* has a chapter on emotional abuse entitled, 'The Bruises Are All on the Inside'.[2] Of course, this could be said of pretty much any adult survivor of any form of child abuse. There is often very little outward sign of the

---

[2] Susan Forward, *Toxic Parents* (New York: Bantam, 2002).

traumatic history that survivors are carrying. In a way this highlights the fact that where there is any form of abuse, it is likely that there will be emotional abuse present as well.

Physical abuse

Physical abuse is just what it sounds like. It's when an adult deliberately causes physical pain to a child. That includes things like hitting, kicking, punching, slapping, smacking, pinching and shaking. It can also include using heat, cold, wetness or dirt to cause physical discomfort. It can include using physical objects to cause a child pain – for example sticks, belts, shoes, sharp things such as needles or pins. It could also include using substances to cause pain or discomfort to the child and/or gratification to the adult – for example, drugs, alcohol, prescription or over-the-counter medications, other poisonous or noxious substances, human waste.

Sometimes the physical abuse of children is made to seem more palatable by calling it *strict discipline* or *corporal punishment*, or some other euphemism. We also need to acknowledge that there are cultures in which some degree of physical abuse of children by adults is considered acceptable. Within my own lifetime it was considered not only acceptable but normal for teachers to have the power to beat a child with a stick, strap or shoe as a form of 'discipline'. Fortunately, that has now been made illegal. However, some groups within society still believe it is acceptable for parents to beat their children in the form of smacking or slapping, and the right to do so as a means of discipline, as long as no injury or mark is inflicted, is still protected in English law.

It is probably important that we try to have some understanding for those parents and teachers, particularly from an older generation who were brought up to believe that this was an acceptable form of discipline, and who tried to use it sparingly and with restraint. We should not necessarily stigmatise them as child-battering monsters. However, we also need to be clear that this is no longer acceptable. There are numerous studies now that show the long-term damage that comes from children being 'disciplined' by the use of physical pain. In the end, however some people may try to justify it, an adult inflicting physical pain or discomfort on a child, whether for their own gratification, out of anger, or in the name of 'discipline', is physically abusing that child.[3]

Sexual abuse

Sexual abuse includes a huge range of acts perpetrated by adults on children, aimed at providing the adults with sexual gratification. As well as penetrative intercourse of all sorts, it includes engaging in inappropriate touch, exposing children to sexual acts between adults, exposing children to pornography, using children to produce pornography, inciting children to carry out sexual acts with other children, engaging in sexual dialogue in online forums and chat rooms, sending or soliciting text messages with sexual content with children. The list is pretty disgusting, but it could go on and on.

---

[3] Proverbs 13:24 refers to discipline and correction in a general sense – the word for 'rod' is the same as that used in Psalm 23:4 – as a means of guiding a flock of sheep, rather than as a specific means of corporal punishment.

It is important to make it very clear that just because a child or young person does not resist or object, or even if they give verbal consent to sexual activity with an adult, it is still abuse. Many victims of sexual abuse do not resist or object. They may give verbal agreement, and may appear to cooperate with the acts they are being made or encouraged to perform. However, the imbalance of power created by the difference in ages means that it is impossible for a child to give *informed consent* to sexual activity with an adult.

The effects of child sexual abuse on children and over the longer term upon adult survivors is particularly corrosive and damaging. There are a number of reasons for this, which we will explore in later chapters, but the basic reason is that our culture attaches shame and stigma to sexual activity, while at the same time promoting it as highly desirable. This cultural mixed message, which children learn very early, creates the potential for great confusion, damage and shame.

The impact of trauma

Childhood abuse has an impact on us in all sorts of different ways. However, there is also a knock-on impact, and in a very real way, the effects of trauma ripple out from the survivor, affecting family, friends, work colleagues and society as a whole.

Just thinking about the impact on mental and physical health, more than 70 million work days are lost every year because of mental health problems, rising to 90 million when stress-related physical ailments are included. Now, of course, not all mental health problems are related to

46

childhood abuse, but even at a very conservative estimate the effects of childhood trauma on health run to *billions* of pounds every year.[4]

So just how severe is the wider impact of childhood abuse? We are going to take a quick look at four key areas, and how they relate to childhood abuse.

Mental health issues

Perhaps the most obvious area in which child abuse and other trauma has an impact is mental health. There is solid research to show that those who have experienced abuse as children, or any form of complex trauma, are far more likely to be diagnosed with a whole range of mental health problems. Up to 60 per cent of adults accessing mental health treatment in the UK report having been abused or maltreated as children.[5]

There are of course some mental health problems that are recognised as being directly linked to trauma in general. The most well-known of these is post-traumatic stress disorder (PTSD). However, specialist treatment for PTSD is hard to access, and in particular there is very little treatment provision for the complex variety, CPTSD which is linked to childhood abuse and other severe trauma. There are also a number of specific mental health problems linked to trauma that are known as dissociative disorders. These are frequently undiagnosed and many mental health

[4] G Conti, et al, 'The Economic Cost of Child Maltreatment in the UK: A Preliminary Study' (London: NSPCC, 2017).
[5] Anne Lazenbatt, 'The impact of abuse and neglect on the health and mental health of children and young people',
https://www.choiceforum.org/docs/impactabuse.pdf (accessed 4th February 2018).

professionals have no training in either recognising or treating them. We will be looking in depth at dissociation and its links with abuse in a later chapter.

One of the effects that a traumatic experience has on us is to flood our bodies and brains with difficult-to-handle emotions – primarily fear, but also anger and sadness. When our trauma is severe or repeated, as it often is when we have been abused as children, it knocks our body and mind's systems for keeping our emotions stable offline. As a result we struggle to regulate our moods. This means that the overwhelming majority of us will struggle with things such as anxiety or depression at some point in our adult lives. Even at a less obvious level, almost all of us experience difficulties with things such as low self-esteem and lack of confidence. Anxiety and depression are generally seen as being at the lower end of the scale of severity in terms of mental health. However, it is worth being aware that more workdays are lost to these issues than to any other physical or mental health causes. In addition, what are sometimes called 'mood disorders' account for a phenomenal number of prescriptions issued by doctors. The most recent figures show that in the UK there are more than four million long-term users of antidepressant medication, with 1.6 million people being prescribed antidepressants for the first time in 2017.[6]

---

[6] Pamela Duncan and Nicola Davis, 'Four Million People in England are Long-term Users of Antidepressants',
https://www.theguardian.com/society/2018/aug/10/four-million-people-in-england-are-long-term-users-of-antidepressants (accessed 10th August 2018).

At what is sometimes considered to be the more severe end of the scale, when we have been abused or traumatised over a long period of time, the disruption to our ways of processing feelings and thoughts can lead to us having some major mental health problems. These would include things such as bipolar disorder, various personality disorders, and schizophrenia. Exact figures are hard to obtain, in part because accounts of childhood abuse are often discounted by mental health professionals as either being delusions or attention seeking. However, if we just take two of the more common mental 'disorders' we discover some very striking figures. For example, it is estimated that more than 90 per cent of people with borderline personality disorder have experienced abuse or other severe trauma as children.[7] To give another example, where people have experienced complex trauma over a long period of time, they can be up to fifty times more likely to develop a psychotic condition later in life.[8]

I should probably say at this point that I and many others working with adult survivors believe that the prevailing models of mental health diagnosis and treatment in the UK and much of the developed Western world are not really fit for purpose when it comes to helping survivors of complex trauma and abuse. The biomedical model, as it is known, views mental health

[7] Charlotte Jackson, 'Personality Disorders: A Trauma Perspective', https://bcnpa.org/personality-disorders-a-trauma-perspective/ (accessed 12th April 2019).

[8] Alok Jha, 'Severe Abuse in Childhood May Treble Risk of Schizophrenia', https://www.theguardian.com/science/2012/apr/18/severe-abuse-childhood-risk-schizophrenia (accessed 21st February 2015).

problems as being *diseases*, which have their origins in some as yet undiscovered genetic predisposition, or in other neurochemical imbalances of mysterious origin. The model works on the assumption that these *mental disorders* are for the most part lifelong conditions that can be treated and managed with medication, but which in all likelihood cannot be cured. This is not the place for a full discussion of this debate, but it is important for us to be aware that survivors who seek mainstream treatment for mental health issues are unlikely to find help that is appropriate and adequate. My own view is that while there may be a role for the short-term use of some psychiatric medications – especially those that help to regulate mood – most of the long-term treatments available are of little benefit, and may actively be harmful, to already vulnerable survivors of trauma.

Furthermore, it is unhelpful to view trauma and its long-lasting effects in terms of an illness or a disease. Trauma, and especially childhood abuse, is an *injury* inflicted deliberately by others. Understanding this is vital to those recovering from trauma. One of the most damaging effects of childhood abuse in particular is that often those of us who have been victims blame ourselves in some way for what has happened to us. If we are able to view the abuse we suffered as having caused emotional and psychological injuries, it helps us to assign responsibility for our distress, where it rightly belongs – with those who traumatised us.

Addiction and compulsive behaviours
Many of us who have been abused as children at some point feel that we need to do something to help us manage

our emotions. Some of us get intoxicated, primarily because at least to begin with it makes us feel better. It changes our emotional state. It can lift our moods when we are depressed. It can take the edge off our anxiety. It can numb the pain of grief or keep us distant from the memories of trauma. It can even help us feel more confident and likeable. The fact that these things are a very temporary sticking plaster over the problem, not to mention rather unpredictable in their effects, makes no difference. We are all too often tormented by our feelings and our memories. The attraction of a drink, a pill, something to smoke or snort, even an injection to numb the pain and bring the feelings and memories under control, no matter how temporary that control might be, is pretty obvious. It is hardly surprising therefore to discover that more than 40 per cent of dependent drug users also meet the diagnostic criteria for PTSD.[9]

There are various ways of looking at addiction. Some people see drug misuse as a criminal issue. Others see it as a mental health problem. Still others see it as evidence of social dysfunction. There may be some truth in all of these, but for abuse survivors, drug and alcohol use is best seen as an attempt to self-medicate our distress and pain.

Of course, that type of self-medication isn't limited to getting drunk or out of it on drugs. It is a similar process when we get caught up with other compulsive behaviours – food, gambling, self-harm, even eating disorders. Food first excites and then sedates us. Gambling gives us a buzz,

[9] E Papastavrou, et al, 'Co-morbidity of Post-Traumatic Stress Disorders and Substance Misuse Disorder' (*Health Science Journal*, Volume 5, Issue 2, 2011).

especially when we're winning. Self-harm, for some of us, relieves tension and other distressing feelings (though we need to be aware that there may be other reasons for self-harming behaviour as well). Eating disorders, though they are very complex in themselves, are very often a way for us to feel in control when everything else feels out of control.

The problem with all addictions and compulsive behaviours is that although they may start out as a way to manage and control the pain and distress we feel, eventually the danger is that they themselves become out of control and unmanageable. Instead of providing a solution to the pain and the distress, they become another source of pain and distress. We end up with survivors, who already feel they are somehow wrong or to blame for the things that happened to them and their inability to move on from the long-term effects, now having another stick with which to beat themselves – yet another reason to believe that they are of no value or worth.

Physical health issues

The link between childhood abuse and mental health difficulties is perhaps one that most people would expect, but what is perhaps not quite so obvious is the link between trauma and physical health. Nevertheless, we probably should expect this to be the case. There has been evidence for many, many years of a connection between significant life events and physical ill health, even for adults. It is now widely acknowledged that a number of common physical complaints are at least in part stress related. The reality is that our minds – our emotions, our thoughts and our beliefs – write deeply on our bodies.

Traumatic events and our responses to them over the long term cause our system to be flooded with various chemicals – most notably *adrenaline* and *cortisol* – which can have a profound effect on our physical organs. Over time, overproduction of these stress chemicals within the body can be a major factor in a number of physical conditions. Not only does the abuse make it more likely that we will develop physical health problems in the first place, it also means that we take longer to recover than those who were not abused as children.

The effect of childhood abuse can be seen right across the spectrum of physical health. It places stress on the cardiovascular system – the heart, lungs and circulation – leading to higher rates of heart disease, circulatory disease and respiratory problems among survivors. Trauma also has an impact on the autoimmune system. Sometimes it can lower our immune system, meaning that we are more susceptible to conditions such as colds, flu and sore throats, not to mention more serious conditions such as sepsis. Slightly paradoxically, at other times trauma can have the opposite effect, and send the autoimmune system into a hyperalert state, which can in turn mean that we are more likely to develop inflammatory conditions such as arthritis, psoriasis, irritable bowel syndrome and many others. The heightened immune response also means that we are more likely than others to develop a range of allergies.

There are also a number of conditions for which we don't necessarily understand the mechanism or the link with trauma. However, research indicates that trauma survivors are more likely to develop these health issues.

They include some types of seizure, various chronic conditions such as ME/chronic fatigue syndrome and fibromyalgia, and even some types of cancer. In fact, it is probably in some of these long-term, chronic physical conditions that the effect of trauma in particular is most evident. As if the original pain and distress caused by the abuse we experienced were not enough, survivors of abuse are far more likely than those who were not abused to develop a long-term physical health condition at some point in their lives.[10]

As both a therapist and a survivor, I have found it helpful to look at some of these physical conditions in symbolic ways. For me it began when I had a year in which it seemed that I caught a cold pretty much every month. Although none of the illnesses were serious, my therapist at the time suggested that the constant colds, with the runny nose and watery eyes, might be a way of my body shedding the tears I didn't want to. We began to look at the things in my life that were causing unexpressed sadness, and within weeks the colds went away. I have experienced two long-term chronic illnesses in my life, both of which seem to be related to trauma. The first was when I developed ME/chronic fatigue syndrome in my mid-thirties. The second was when I developed psoriasis in my late forties. Both of these can helpfully be thought about in symbolic ways. With ME the body experiences a loss of physical power for no apparent reason. Moving about, walking, standing, and even engaging in conversation can

[10] 'About the CDC–Kaiser ACE Study',
https://www.cdc.gov/violenceprevention/childabuseandneglect/acestudy/about.html (accessed 3rd March 2019).

all become incredibly fatiguing and painful. I am one of the fortunate ones who recovered from ME, but it made me wonder if that loss of physical power might in some way be connected to the sense of powerlessness I felt as a child when I was being abused over many years. I still have psoriasis, which is an autoimmune disease in which the body overproduces skin cells to form thick scaly patches on the body. It started at a time when I was under huge pressure from two directions. Firstly, I was carrying an enormous caseload of very complex clients, including many survivors of abuse. Secondly, in my own therapy I was finally beginning to work through some of the worst elements of the abuse I had experienced as a child. Our skin, to a certain extent, protects us from the world. It seems to me that my autoimmune system is constantly attempting to create a thicker barrier between me and the world in order to provide some sort of protection from the effects of abuse – either my own or that of others.

When survivors experience serious or chronic illnesses, or even sometimes minor illnesses, it may be helpful for us to ask ourselves this question, *What is my body trying to tell me about myself, my history or my life, that my mind doesn't want to recognise?*

In some ways it isn't easy to talk about the connection between trauma and physical health without scaremongering. It is important to be aware of it, but at the same time we don't want to cause needless anxiety. It is important that we understand that though risks of developing physical health problems are increased among survivors, this doesn't mean that such problems are inevitable or even likely. Looking at it from the other end, we also need to be clear that simply because someone develops an autoimmune disease (to give one example) it does not necessarily mean that person has a history of childhood abuse or other trauma.

Relational difficulties
The last broad area of impact I want to look at for now is the effect of trauma on relational difficulties. This is going to be a very quick overview, because relationships for survivors of abuse can be a particularly problematic area, and so gets a whole chapter to itself. However, it is worth being aware in a general sense of how the abuse we experienced can affect us and our relationships.

One of the factors that makes child abuse so damaging is that the overwhelming majority takes place within the family or within a circle of trusted friends and associates. Such a betrayal of trust directly attacks our sense of self – who we see ourselves to be and how we feel about ourselves. In addition, it also undermines our perception of other people. Others may often come to be seen as either actively dangerous to us, or at least as untrustworthy or uncaring. As such, abuse does enormous damage to the ways in which we relate to other people, and the effects of that damage can continue throughout our lives.

As a result, we often experience high levels of isolation and loneliness, and struggle to make and maintain meaningful or healthy friendships. We may also experience high levels of social anxiety, and find it difficult to function appropriately in social situations. Typically, survivors will also be more likely to form unstable relationships, particularly close relationships. We sometimes fall into a pattern in which we form intense and close relationships relatively quickly, but then find those relationships disrupted by arguments and falling out. In terms of intimate relationships and marriage, survivors of abuse tend to experience a higher level of relational and marital breakdown than others.

However, it is important not to stereotype. It is tempting to think of all survivors as being withdrawn, introverted loners. But the reality is that we can't be boxed up so easily. Some of us are just as likely to be outgoing, extroverted party animals, who have a compulsive need for connection with other people to distract us from our unacknowledged pain and distress.

Simple and complex trauma

Some people categorise trauma as being either *simple* or *complex*. However, these are not either/or categories. Most people's experience of trauma exists somewhere on a spectrum between the two extremes. What is true, however, is that the degree to which people are affected by the long-term impact of trauma is largely related to how complex their traumatic experiences have been.

It probably doesn't take a genius to work out that when we have been abused as children – deliberately made the target of mistreatment – the impact on us is likely to be considerably more complex than the impact of trauma that was caused accidentally or incidentally. That is not to minimise the distress and pain felt by those who have suffered those other forms of trauma. We are not talking about severity here. Simple trauma can be just as severe in terms of the level of distress it causes, but the impact tends to be less complicated both in terms of how we as survivors understand and process it, and the twists and turns of our journey of healing and recovery.

There are a number of factors that increase the degree of complexity and we are going to take a quick look at these.

Frequency

The first factor is *frequency*. As a rough rule of thumb, the more abuse we suffer, the more complex the trauma, and the more impact it is going to have on us over time. When we are abused on a single occasion, it may be very unpleasant indeed, but because that experience exists on its own, in the middle of a life filled with more positive experiences, our minds have a chance to process it and will tend over time to categorise it as an isolated incident. By itself it isn't going to set a pattern for our lives or define completely who we see ourselves to be.

Just to be really clear, this is not to minimise the distress that a single abusive incident can cause. The effects are still going to be extremely painful, and we are still going to need help to recover. However, the recovery is likely to be more straightforward and of relatively short duration. If, on the other hand, we have already been abused once, and then have subsequent experiences of abuse, it tends to shift the way we see ourselves and the world around us. It becomes harder for our minds to categorise the abuse as an isolated incident. Rather, our mind does one of the things it is very good at and starts trying to make a pattern out of what has happened. It's a way in which we can try to make a scary world just a bit more predictable. That pattern becomes a filter for how we see ourselves and the rest of the world. The world is no longer an intrinsically safe place, in which the odd isolated traumatic thing may happen. We start to see it as an intrinsically unsafe place in which abuse and other trauma seems increasingly likely.

Furthermore, once we have experienced the emotional and psychological injury caused by being abused once, our resilience to subsequent events becomes weaker.

I worked with a survivor who had been sexually and emotionally abused many times in childhood. With help she was making good progress in her recovery, but then one morning on the way to work she was involved in a serious car accident. Even though she walked away more or less physically uninjured, she had an extremely strong post-traumatic stress reaction to the accident, and the impact on her was far greater than might have been expected under other circumstances. This was because although the car crash was a trauma totally unrelated to the abuse she suffered as a child, it reinforced her pattern of viewing the world as an inherently unsafe place, and viewing herself as someone to whom unsafe things happened.

Age

The second factor that helps to determine the complexity of traumatic experiences is *age*, Again, as a rough rule of thumb, we can say that the younger we were when we were first abused, the more complex the impact of that trauma is likely to be on us.

The reason for this is that our identity, our personality and our patterns of thinking feeling and relating, as well as our defensive and coping mechanisms, all develop quite slowly over time. In the very earliest stages of life we are wholly dependent on other people to give us appropriate care and nurturing. This makes us very vulnerable to any experiences that run counter to our needs.

Of course, all children have negative experiences – things that cause them discomfort, pain or fear. But if these are appropriately handled by caregivers, then the child recovers quickly and no damage is done. In fact, such experiences, along with being given the appropriate care and nurturing to recover, are an essential part of a child's early development. They help us to build resilience, and allow us to learn how to categorise experiences as safe or unsafe.

For example, if when we were very small we were frightened by a dog that barked and jumped up at us, we didn't have the experience or the mental capacity to realise that the dog may in fact merely have been trying to be friendly. But if we were soothed and reassured by a caregiver, and if the dog calmed down and we were introduced properly to it, the chances are that we would overcome our fear, and we might even come to relate to that dog and other dogs in a positive way.

However, it doesn't always work out so well. This happened once with a survivor I was working with. When she was little and a dog jumped at her and barked loudly, she was not soothed and reassured, but was instead called derogatory names, and the dog was goaded to bark and jump up even more, for the amusement of her parents. This was a terrifying and abusive traumatic experience for her, and it is hardly surprising that after this she had a very negative reaction to dogs, even small and very friendly ones, that lasted into adulthood. More than that, however, this and other similar experiences have embedded in her mind a fearful filter on the world. Anything that is new, unusual or startling causes her to panic. This is complex, because there is no obvious link between a new person starting in the office at work and her fear. It doesn't seem reasonable that she treats her new colleague as if they were a potential threat to her life. It only makes sense when we understand that her basic ways of relating to new and unexpected events are rooted in genuinely terrifying experiences prior to the age of three.

This is not to say that if we began being abused when we were older that it didn't damage us. It most certainly did. However, the age at which we were first abused does mean we respond differently and perhaps with a different type of complexity, particularly with regard to the long-term impact. Generally speaking, if we were abused prior to school age, the effects are likely to be more complex, and still more complex if the abuse started earlier than the age of three. However, there are many other factors involved in determining just how complex our responses to the trauma of abuse are likely to be.

Multiplicity of types

The third factor that determines the complexity of trauma arising from abuse is what might be called *multiplicity of types*. What I mean by this is that the more types of abuse we experienced, the more complex the trauma and our responses to it are likely to be. So, for example, a person who has experienced any single type of abuse will sustain trauma, and that trauma is likely to be serious and distressing in its effects. However, if we were subjected to neglect *and* emotional abuse *and* physical abuse *and* sexual abuse, it is pretty obvious that being abused in these multiple ways means we are going to be impacted in lots of different ways. The assault on who we are is going to have come through many different channels. Our reactions to what happened to us are therefore going to be much more complex.

I want to be really careful how I say this, because the last thing I want is for those survivors who have experienced a single form of abuse to think that somehow their pain and distress is less important or carries less weight than that of someone who has experienced multiple forms of abuse. There is no hierarchy of pain and distress. We are not talking here about severity of experience, but about the complexity of the post-traumatic reactions. The pain and distress felt by a survivor of one type of child abuse may be as great or greater than that felt by a survivor of multiple types of child abuse.

In reality, almost all of us who were abused as children were abused in more than one way. This is because neglect, physical abuse and sexual abuse, in particular if they took place within the family or in a trusted setting, almost always involve some element of emotional abuse, control or manipulation. If they didn't, the perpetrators wouldn't have been able to get away with it. Many of us who were sexually abused as children, whether by a parent or another family member, or by a stranger, have had the experience of not being believed or having the severity of what we suffered dismissed by a 'non-abusive' parent. Such denial and dismissal by those who are supposed to protect us is in itself a form of emotional abuse.

Looked at from the other direction, I have worked with many people who were subjected to emotional abuse but do not necessarily recognise that they were subjected to other forms of abuse as well. Sometimes we experienced physical abuse, but because of the emotional abuse and control, we learned to agree with our abusers that this was just 'strict discipline'. Sometimes, we were exposed to forms of distorted sexualised behaviour, which though they may have stopped short of physical contact were nonetheless abusive – for example, adults who were inappropriately naked around us, or who wanted us to be inappropriately naked around them.

Source

The fourth factor that has an influence on the complexity of the trauma is the *source* – in other words, who perpetrated the abuse. There is a certain irony that the cases of child abuse that receive the most publicity are those in which the perpetrator is a stranger to the victim. The truth is that the overwhelming majority of survivors – between 80 and 90 per cent – were abused within the family or a close circle of friends. By the time we include those perpetrators who are known and trusted by the family in professional roles, the figure rises to more than 95 per cent.[11]

Unsurprisingly, when we were abused by someone known to us, it is going to have a far greater impact than if we were abused by a stranger. Furthermore, if the people who abused us were family members, and in particular parents or other caregivers, this is going to have an even greater impact. This is due to the breach of trust and

---

[11] L Radford et al, 'Child Abuse and Neglect in the UK Today' (London: NSPCC, 2011).

subversion of the usual loving and caregiving roles by the abusers.

As children we are wired not only to need love, affection, care and nurture, but to expect it. When those things were not present, or when instead we received abuse, neglect and violence from those who were supposed to love and care for us, it does huge long-lasting damage to our sense of self, and to our view of close relationships. Children in this position almost always choose to blame themselves for what has happened to them, rather than to blame those who have abused them. In particular when the abusers were close family and caregivers, we were forced to make a terrible choice between believing that we ourselves were bad and deserved of the abuse we received, and believing that our family and caregivers are monstrous, evil people who abused and exploited us for their own gratification. Sadly the innate wiring to love our family and to expect care and love from them usually wins out, leaving us with some incredibly complex, distressing and painful feelings about ourselves and our abusers.

In the interests of clarity, situations in which family members and caregivers may not actively have abused us themselves, but knowingly failed to protect us from abuse by other people, still counts as abuse by a caregiver. As small children we instinctively need and expect that parents and caregivers will protect us from threat and harm, so when they fail to do so, or even make a deliberate choice to put us in harm's way, we feel almost as betrayed and let down as if they themselves had actively abused us.

Again, we are not making any judgement about the severity of the distress that may be felt by the survivor, but acknowledging that the closer relationship the survivor has to those who abused them, the more complex their reactions are likely to be.

Multiplicity of sources

The fifth factor influencing the complexity of trauma and post-traumatic responses is *multiplicity of sources*. What I mean by this is fairly straightforward. When we were abused by more than one person, it greatly increases the complexity of our reactions to what happened to us.

Very often abuse is a crime carried out by one single abuser. However, there are also many situations in which we experienced abuse by more than one person. Sometimes those people may be known to each other, but not always. Unfortunately, one of the things that predators become very adept at is recognising children who are already vulnerable, perhaps because they have already been abused by other people.

My own story is that having been abused by members of my own family and their own circle of friends and acquaintances, I was then subjected to sexual abuse quite independently of them, by a piano teacher. Clearly this man was a predator who somehow recognised that I was already vulnerable because of the abuse I had experienced within my family. Not only did I not resist his actions, I accepted them as being simply one of the normal ways in which I expected adults to relate to children.

In other situations, of course, the different perpetrators are known to each other. Sometimes we were abused by different members of our family, or some of us may have been the victim of some form of organised group, which is a particularly distressing and complex type of abuse.

The multiplicity of sources of abuse contributes to the complexity of the trauma because we get the message and come to believe that this is somehow a common or even normal way for adults to treat children. It distorts our image of adulthood, not only in terms of how we see our abusers, but also how we see other adults. It also distorts how we think and feel about our own future adult selves. It is even possible that some of us when we reach adulthood might view ourselves as being abnormal in some way, because we ourselves do not relate to children in abusive ways.

Severity

The last factor that is sometimes seen as increasing the complexity of trauma is *severity*.

We need to be really careful in how we think about this. As I said earlier, there is no hierarchy of pain and distress. It isn't helpful for us to classify some forms of abuse as being more distressing or painful than others. The danger if we do is that we invalidate something of our own experience – our own pain and distress. This is particularly destructive to us as survivors, because we have already experienced such a high level of invalidation, both through being abused and possibly by being disbelieved, and also by living in a world that really doesn't know how to respond in helpful ways to us and our trauma.

Nevertheless, at the same time there is clearly a sense in which some abuse can be seen as more severe, not just because it causes more in the way of physical damage, but also because there is deliberate intention on the part of the perpetrators to cause the maximum damage and distress that they can.

I have personally experienced and have worked with survivors who have experienced types of abuse that could best be described as deliberate sadistic torture. While not in any way negating the pain and distress experienced by survivors of other forms of abuse, it is undeniable that something about the intention on the part of perpetrators to cause extreme physical or psychological harm introduces new levels of complexity.

My own observation, both from my own life and from working with survivors for almost thirty years, is that these cases of extreme sadistic abuse also have associated with them most of the other factors that contribute to the trauma being more complex. The abuse is almost always frequent. It often started when we were very young. It generally involves more than one type of abuse. It is likely that some of the abusers are close family members. There are almost always more than one, and often many, abusers.

The truth is that all trauma, and certainly all trauma caused by child abuse, is complex to one degree or another. The best approach for us, both as survivors and as those supporting survivors, is to recognise that complexity and learn appropriate ways of navigating our way through it.

Supporter's Pause for Thought: How can I understand?

The one you are supporting is going through things you may never have experienced and can scarcely imagine. There is no shame in not understanding. However, often the gift of love and care you can most easily give is your willingness to learn. Many survivors feel themselves to be unworthy of belonging or even of the simple care of other people. All too often they feel like a non-person. They are like the leper who moved Jesus' heart with compassion:

> Jesus reached out his hand and touched the man. 'I am willing,' he said. 'Be clean!' Immediately he was cleansed of his leprosy.
> *Matthew 8:3*

It doesn't take much on the part of supporters to reach out, to take an interest, to see the person behind the pain, and to show care.

- Is there a book you can read?
- Is there a website you can visit?
- Are there questions you can ask?

Remember the only stupid question is the one you never ask.

Chapter Three
Survivors and the Church

What we hope for

It probably won't come as too much of a surprise that many survivors connect with Christian churches at some point on their journey. What may come as more of a surprise is the large number of survivors who seem to end up struggling with those same churches. Part of the reason for this is that churches offer survivors hope. For those of us who have been abused as children, hope can be something in very short supply. By the time we have made our way into adulthood, sometimes it feels by the skin of our teeth, typically we will be desperate for anything that can hold out hope to us that things could get better.

To the extent the Church is able to deliver on the hope it holds out to us, our relationship with the Christian world is likely to be happy and supportive. To the extent that it fails to do so, our relationship is likely to be problematic. We are going to take a look at the things survivors of abuse are really hoping for from the Church.

Shalom

I've used the Hebrew word *shalom* deliberately. Although it is frequently translated as *peace*, in fact it has a much richer set of connotations. Survivors of abuse generally do not live at peace. We are frequently living in the middle of emotional and spiritual turmoil caused by what happened to us. There are times when our heads are noisy places, with thoughts and feelings all swirling around. It is as if we are trying to find some solid place where we might be able to find our footing and rest for a while.

Churches often offer us that peace, and along with a whole lot more. *Shalom* includes connotations of wholeness and well-being. We know we are not whole. We know that the abuse broke us emotionally, spiritually, sometimes physically. Even our identity can sometimes feel shattered into pieces. We know that all is not well in our being – unlike the famous hymn, we cannot very often say, 'It is Well with My Soul',[12] much though we might like to be able to do so. The hope that a church that follows the Prince of Shalom might be able to offer us wholeness, well-being and rest is very attractive to us.

When I first came to church as an adult survivor, I was desperate for the sort of peace and stability that my life so sorely lacked. After a long time of searching and trying to find something to help me make sense of my very broken life, I began to believe that just possibly in this church full of Christ-following people I could find the thing I was looking for. For me, it all hinged on whether what they were saying about Jesus turned out to be true, and how well they were able to embody that truth.

---

[12] Horatio Spafford, 1828–88.

For survivors of abuse, *shalom* is not optional. Whether we follow Jesus or not, most of us instinctively know that we need that wholeness, peace, well-being and rest. In fact, without those things being present and increasing in our lives, we cannot really say that we are healing from our trauma in any meaningful sense. We look to the Church as the body of Christ, the embodiment on earth of the Prince of Peace, to provide the *shalom* we so desperately need. However, our need for *shalom* is not just an external environmental thing – though there are certainly times when a bit of external peace and quiet can be helpful. Rather, we are looking to the Church as people who can show us how to connect with the source of that peace and wholeness, and how, from the fruit of that connection, we can cultivate an inner wholeness and peace.

Safety

Another thing that is needed by every survivor of abuse is a sense of safety. Of being held securely and protected from whatever might be out there that could cause us harm. It is a need that is totally understandable. Our experience was that we were not safe. At a time when we were unable to protect ourselves, there was insufficient in the way of protection and holding around us to keep us safe. As a result, we were abused and sustained injuries, perhaps to our body, but certainly to our soul – our mind and sense of self.

When I was first connecting with Jesus, I found the stories that most affected me were of Jesus as the good shepherd. The idea that God might be good enough and kind enough to come looking for me, to gather me up when I was absolutely lost in a wilderness of pain and distress, was a deeply powerful one. As was the idea that He was strong enough to keep the thieves, wolves and other predators away from me. My entire life I had been easy pickings for predators of all sorts, and I knew very well that I was incapable of protecting myself from them, or indeed of protecting me from myself. I knew that I needed someone who would find me and gather me in and protect me in a way that no one else had ever done.

Again this is something that the Church offers to us. Church becomes the means by which we can make and deepen our relationship with the shepherd. Church in a sense is the safe sheepfold, the refuge where the shepherd gathers us in. It's a theme that is echoed throughout Scripture – God's people gathered into a place of safety, where they can be safe and flourish. For survivors that is what we want, and what we need to become whole. In a very real sense, we cannot find *shalom* unless at the same time we find a place of safety.

What does a place of safety look like? For most survivors, it is the exact opposite of what we experienced in the situations where we were abused, whether that was in our own families or elsewhere. That means a place of safety is one in which we will not be controlled, manipulated, lied to, lied about, exploited, punished, humiliated, degraded or forced to do things against our conscience – the list could go on. A place of safety is also going to be somewhere where we have positive experiences of some of the key things that were missing in our experience of abuse. This could include being valued, nurtured, listened to, believed, loved unconditionally, and so on.

It is only within such a safe environment that we can really begin to find the peace, wholeness and well-being that are the hallmarks of our recovery from what happened to us.

Community

A third thing that survivors look for as they are on their journey of recovery and healing is community, or perhaps we might call it fellowship. One of the effects of the abuse we experienced is isolation. For reasons we will go into in more detail in another chapter, abuse cuts us off from other people – family, friends, loved ones and the world at large. We isolate ourselves as a way of protecting what is already hurt and broken in us, but the truth is that, like every human being, we have a need to belong and to be included.

Church offers us inclusion and belonging. It opens the door to us and tells us that the Church is our new family. These are our brothers and sisters; they are a ready-made new friendship group that is going to relate to us with the love of Jesus. This is a message that is reinforced by the gospel stories, many of which make it clear that Jesus connects particularly with those who are broken, hurting and on the margins. He does not condemn, but accepts, includes and loves. Our hope is that His people, in the form of the Church, will also respond to us and our brokenness in the same ways.

A sense of community or fellowship is an incredibly powerful and healing thing. It's one of the reasons why twelve-step programmes for addictions, such as Alcoholics Anonymous or Narcotics Anonymous, have had the enduring success that they do. The feeling that we are surrounded by people who love us, and who to a certain extent at least know and share our pain, can do a great deal to help restore our sense of self. It gives us hope that whatever the future might hold for us, we do not have to face it on our own. There are those who will journey with us no matter what happens, so that even when we stumble and fall, there will be people around us ready and willing to help us get to our feet again.

Transformation

Survivors of abuse are looking for change. We want things to be different in our lives, and above all else we want to *be* different. Unfortunately, most survivors do not think much of themselves. We tend to view ourselves in a very negative light, blaming ourselves for the things that happened to us, as well as for the things that go wrong in our lives now. For most of us, there are many things we would change about ourselves if we could, but the problem is we don't know how.

Church offers us a Saviour, whose whole message is one of transformation. The hope that is offered to us is that as we follow Him, our lives will be transformed into something infinitely better. We know it's going to be a journey – there are plenty of Christian clichés about us being a 'work in progress' – but the end result we are assured is that we will become like the One we follow. The way we learn to do this is by following the teachings of the Church and its leaders, and by staying connected to the body of believers. The specifics of what that might look like will vary widely between different churches and denominations, but we are assured that if we remain faithful to Christ, and faithful to His Church, we will make it in the end.

That 'making it in the end' includes an assurance of a final transformation after death, for those who are in Christ. This is a transformation that lasts beyond the limited time and space of our lives, and includes an eternal enfolding into the love and identity of Christ.

That hope of transformation – of being able to change – is very attractive to survivors, in particular because there is often the suggestion from churches that the long process of change, recovery and healing can be supernaturally shortened. We are told that God has the power to heal us far more quickly and efficiently than any human endeavour. For those of us who are wrestling with the pain and distress of recovery, the idea that God can change things, and change us, in the blink of an eye, is surely something worth hoping for?

The unfortunate reality

It's a weekday lunchtime, and I am sitting at my desk writing up some notes. The phone rings. An unfamiliar number, but I pick it up anyway. It's one of the pastoral team at a local church, and they want to talk to me about a client they recently referred to me.

'We had an incident during the Sunday meeting. She got very upset by something, and started crying, but when people tried to pray for her she started yelling and screaming abuse at them, and telling them to get away from her. It's not the first time we've had problems with her. She's very attention seeking and needy, always creating a drama. So manipulative and controlling too. If everything doesn't go her way she kicks off and causes disruption. We want to help her, but we really can't tolerate this sort of behaviour. It's upsetting the other members. I've told her

if she doesn't pull herself together she's going to need to find another church.'

I try to be kind and patient. I remind myself that most people don't know how to cope with people in deep distress. I try to explain that though I'm not sure what triggered my client and caused her to become so distressed, there will have been something, even though it was probably unintentional. I try to explain that having people crowd around her when she is upset, and even worse put their hands on her as they pray, will most likely cause her to have a panic attack, due to the echoes it has with past abuse. I don't think it's doing much good.

'Well, we just wanted to warn you,' the pastor continues. 'You need to watch out that she doesn't end up manipulating you. We're certainly not going to put up with it here for much longer.'

I manage to thank him for his concern and stay civil until the call is over. What I want to do is put my head in my hands in despair. This is the third such conversation I've had this week, and although I try to remind myself that they mean well, the temptation to give these people a piece of my mind is almost overwhelming.

This may not necessarily be a typical example of the interaction between survivors of abuse and their church. However, in my experience, similar reactions are unfortunately all too common. Good and well-meaning Christian people can feel overwhelmed by the needs of survivors. Perhaps they don't feel equipped to meet the needs of those who are in pain and distress. Sadly, this can cause even mature Christians and leaders in some churches to lose sight of the heart of Jesus for the lost, the broken and the hurting. It can sometimes feel easier to default to dealing with survivors and their complex needs in ways that are somewhat legalistic and judgemental.

Unfortunately, the reality is that the relationship between survivors and the Church is not always quite as smooth and as hope filled as we might like it to be. In fact, at times it may seem as if the Church, rather than being the promised and sought-after source of hope for survivors, may actually become part of the problem, rather than part of the solution.

It is probably fair to say that most churches and church leaders do not intend to cause problems for survivors. Most people are essentially well-meaning, and want to help those who are struggling if they can. The difficulty is that most people simply do not know how to help in effective ways. When those who are trying to help feel overwhelmed, it can be very tempting to shift the blame on to those they are trying to help. This isn't limited to churches; there are whole schools of psychotherapy that have a similar tendency. However understandable and common it may be, it is still not an acceptable way to go about things. All the more so in a church that is supposed to be offering a place of refuge, healing and transformation to those who are broken.

The not so good news

Some of the difficulty may arise because there are strands within the body of Christ that seem to have an incomplete understanding of the good news. The real good news is of a God who so loves the world, including all the broken people in it, that He sends His own son – the perfect and

77

complete manifestation of Himself – to take on flawed and fallible human flesh and blood. He sends Christ to model wholeness, and to call every broken and misaligned thing back into full connection with the One who is the source of our being – the very embodiment of love and truth. He sends Jesus to move us beyond ways of relating to God that rely on laws, rules and rituals, but which depend solely on the love He has towards us, finding a loving response in our own hearts.

The other version, the one I call the *not so good news*, is different. It seems still to be rooted in the old covenant of law; based on rules, regulations and human effort to be good. It is a version in which God only loves those who show themselves worthy by believing the 'correct' doctrines and behaving in the right ways. The not so good news may have a lot to say about creation and the end times, or about sin and bad behaviour, but it seems to have little to say about love and grace. Where it does talk about love and grace, the not so good news appears to mean something rather different from the simple unconditional love and free grace of the real good news. The not so good version talks a lot about loving the sinner but hating the sin, but looks rather like keeping the sinner at a suitable distance so we don't get contaminated, while telling them that this is love. The not so good news sometimes seems to come up with all sorts of interpretations of Scripture that result in more and more rules to govern every aspect of our lives. At the same time it sometimes seems to ignore many of the things Jesus actually said.

The result of the not so good news is that many of us who are still struggling with the effects of childhood abuse find in our churches, not places of refuge and hope, but a maze of rules and customs that all serve to convince us of something we always suspected anyway – that we are not worthy of love and belonging. We are not worthy of the love of God's people, and in all probability we are not worthy of God's love either.

This is a tragedy. It runs so contrary to the reality of the real good news. Jesus was radically inclusive. He included all those whom the orthodox religion of the day excluded: sick people, sex workers, Samaritans (who were generally considered to be heretics), the hated tax collectors, lepers, those labelled as sinners, and demon possessed. Surely His Church today can find a way to include and support those broken by childhood abuse? I believe that most churches actually do want to serve and support survivors of abuse. I am also sure that there are some churches who do that very well. There are others, however, who perhaps want to support survivors, but don't know how. For these, there are some big challenges to face and overcome.

The first and most important of these challenges isn't new. It has been going on since Jesus Himself took on the legalism and self-righteousness of the Pharisees, and since Paul and others in the early Church had to struggle to keep the fledgling Christian communities free of the influence of those who wanted a return to the Mosaic Law. It is simply this. The Church has to start believing that Jesus actually meant what He said. That the loving character of God is shown more in the stories of the prodigal son, the good Samaritan and the Beatitudes (to mention just three passages) than it is in Old-Testament-style legalism and religion. That Jesus, through His incarnation, life, death and resurrection, really has fulfilled and therefore superseded and made obsolete the entire old covenant, and that we are now living in an era of grace, where belonging to Him and His people does not depend on behaviour or external appearances.

If churches can start from that point and keep it central to their teachings and practice, it makes it far easier for them to love and help those who, because of the emotional wounds caused by childhood abuse, may not quite fit the image of the happy and generally sorted Christian.

Misconceptions and misunderstandings

Any church that does not fully embrace the real good news is inevitably going to labour under the burden of a whole number of misconceptions and misunderstandings about survivors of trauma and abuse. This is not because the leaders or the people in those churches are necessarily wanting to be unkind. On the contrary, many of them may well desire to help survivors and see them come to a place of wholeness. It is simply that believing the not so good news means they view the world and survivors through a particular set of coloured lenses.

Here are some of the most common misconceptions and misunderstandings that survivors face in the Church.

Challenging behaviour

When I was a new Christian I struggled with anger. I really wanted to behave and be as good and holy as all the other proper Christians, but I found that from time to time, in the most inappropriate of settings – like the middle of a prayer meeting – something would rise up in me and the next thing I knew I was having an outburst of temper, often accompanied by swearing a great deal and sometimes by storming off. It never lasted long. Usually within a few minutes I had calmed down and was left feeling deeply ashamed and wondering what on earth had just happened. I know there were many others who found my behaviour pretty challenging, and the church leaders were very gracious in trying to understand and help me. But both they and I struggled when they asked what it was I was angry about. Most of the time I had no idea, or the thing I thought I was angry about seemed so trivial.

The thing is, what neither I nor they fully appreciated was that I was being triggered. Because as a child I was sometimes abused in group settings, there were moments when being in a confined space with a number of people – and sometimes the noise levels were just too much – triggered an intense panic reaction. The anger I displayed was more of a reaction to my internal terror than to any real external provocation.

The reality is that life is challenging for many survivors of abuse. It is therefore hardly surprising that our responses to things can sometimes be challenging to the people around us. So much of our behaviour is at least partially driven by unconscious, and frequently uncontrollable, responses to the trauma we experienced. Most survivors of abuse will be triggered and experience out-of-control feelings from time to time. We may experience overwhelming sadness or fear, and react by collapsing into tears, by becoming verbally aggressive, or by running away.

Many of us missed out on the love, affection and affirmation we needed as children. As adults, we may respond by attaching ourselves to anyone who shows us any of those things. This in turn can lead to us becoming quite clingy or dependent, or intruding into people's lives. If those things aren't available to us, we may find it hard to let go of our other sources of comfort, which could include all sorts of behaviour most churches frown on – drinking, overeating, gambling, compulsive shopping, taking drugs, using pornography, compulsive masturbation, engaging in casual sex, etc.

The temptation is for churches simply to view these types of behaviours as 'sinful' and expect people to change their ways in order fully to belong. We end up in a situation where we as survivors really do want to change. We pray prayers of repentance, and we ask people to hold us accountable, and perhaps for a while things improve. But sooner or later, we are triggered again, or life becomes too stressful for us to deal with, and we slip back into our old responses and coping mechanisms. Only this time we have the added shame of failure, and the growing suspicion that maybe we are not acceptable to God after all, because we are not good enough to stop sinning. We end up in a vicious spiral. The more we do this stuff, the more shame we feel and the more we see it as a matter of wilful sin that we could change if we really wanted to, so the less acceptable we feel to God, the less we feel we belong in the church, and the worse we feel about ourselves and the more likely we are to be triggered or resort to our habitual coping mechanisms.

The problem is that the Church has largely misunderstood what sin actually is. The word used for sin in the Gospels actually translates as *missing the mark* and has the implication of being out of alignment. As survivors, we are of course *out of alignment* – that is the effect of the injuries that have been done to us. When we have an injured leg, we walk with a limp. When we have a head injury, our minds don't work the way they should. But abuse causes injuries to the soul – our mind, our emotions and even our sense of self. So it is hardly surprising that our responses and behaviours are out of alignment with what is necessarily most helpful for us. But this isn't something that should cause us to feel shame or to be punished or ostracised. Rather it is something that points to things that need healing.

Real repentance

Very much linked with how the Church deals with challenging behaviour from survivors of abuse is the need for repentance. But how we understand repentance can have a great impact on survivors of abuse. It is probably true to say that for the most part, the Church understands repentance as being some expression of sorrow for our sins. The belief is that as we express sorrow for our bad behaviour or attitudes, God will enable us by the power of the Holy Spirit to change our ways.

As we have already seen in terms of the way that churches all too often deal with challenging behaviour, anything around sin has the potential to be problematic for survivors recovering from childhood abuse. The danger always is that if we feel sorrow for our behaviour or attitudes and then find ourselves slipping into the same behaviours again, we feel condemned and perhaps unworthy of God's help to change. The net result is that we feel more disempowered, more unworthy and more hopeless than we did before. But as we have already seen, much of the 'sinful' behaviour stems from our response to the soul injuries caused by the abuse we have suffered. Surely there has to be a way of thinking about sin and repentance that does not lead to survivors feeling ever more condemned and hopeless?

The original Greek word used in the Gospels for repentance is *metanoia*, which literally means a change of mind and heart. One of the things that is always striking about the ministry of Jesus is that He always sees in people the things they don't see in themselves. Whether it is a rough and ready Galilean fisherman with a bad temper and poor impulse control (Peter), a crazed prostitute (Mary Magdalene), a heretic with poor choice in men (the Samaritan woman at the well) or a murderous Pharisee (Paul), He sees them not as these things, but as who they were created to be. Over time spent with Jesus, either in the flesh or as His disciples after His ascension, all of these people gradually come to have a changed view of themselves. They no longer see themselves as they once were, but as they were born to be. Their minds and hearts have undergone a process of *metanoia* or repentance, so that now, their view of themselves lines up with God's view of them.

This is the true meaning of repentance, when our hearts and minds come back into alignment with God's heart and mind – about ourselves, about Him, and about the world. If we remember that 'sin' is essentially a matter of being out of alignment with God, then clearly this coming back into alignment is how we deal with sin. If we think of ourselves as unworthy, miserable sinners, the chances are we are going to behave in ways that are out of alignment with who God says we are. But as our hearts and minds are healed up and brought back into alignment, the chances are that we begin to behave in ways that accord with who God says we are.

When we view it in this way, repentance is entwined with our own journey of recovery and healing from abuse. As we gradually heal and are made whole, so our behaviour begins to change.

Forgiveness is a journey

As survivors we are often taught by the Church that we need to forgive the people who abused us. In fact, there are inner-healing ministries that would go so far as to say that any significant healing is impossible if we do not first forgive the people who hurt us. It may well be true that coming to a place where we can forgive and release the people who abused us is an important part of our healing journey. However, unless we are very clear about exactly what forgiveness means, and how and when we can most helpfully forgive, the effect on us can be deeply damaging.

Forgiveness, for abuse survivors, is not simple or straightforward. If we try to forgive in a simplistic way it can reinforce some of the toxic messages that we received from our abusers. It can, for example, reinforce the message that our pain and distress is not important. It can give the impression that the abuse we experienced was a minor matter – something trivial and not to make a fuss about. It can encourage us to believe that we have to take responsibility for our abusers rather than looking after ourselves. All of these, and many other possible toxic messages we can receive from being made to 'forgive' before we are ready, combine to confirm the core belief that many survivors of abuse have – that we are not worthy of being loved, looked after, protected and cared for.

Clearly this is not acceptable, and in all honesty I don't believe that most people urging survivors to forgive their abusers would actually want to reinforce such beliefs. Nevertheless, unless we are very careful in talking about forgiveness and how to go about it, that is exactly what will happen. I see a number of survivors who have been through this kind of inner-healing ministry. They rather plaintively report that they have done their best to forgive their abusers, but they are still troubled by all the after-effects of the trauma they suffered, and when they think about their abusers it is with fear, anger and revulsion. I cannot tell you the number of times I have seen survivors in tears, because they are convinced they are headed for hell, simply because they still have these reactions to those who abused them. I believe there are a number of things that can help us understand what forgiveness really means, both for us as survivors and for those who support survivors.

The first is simply this, that forgiveness is a journey not an event. We are sometimes told *forgiveness is a decision*, but that really reduces forgiveness to a mental choice that doesn't involve the heart. But for forgiveness to have any real meaning, it has to involve our hearts. Scripture tells us that God is interested in our hearts, what we feel and believe in our deepest selves. Child abuse breaks our hearts. We are left wounded and injured in our innermost being. This means that for forgiveness to be real it has to be something that is intimately bound up in the healing of our hearts. That healing of hearts does not happen in an instant. It takes time. Recovery from the awful things that happened to us as children can take a considerable length of time, because it involves unravelling all the coping strategies and defences that we have built up to protect ourselves. All this, before we get to deal with any of the actual abusive experiences. As our hearts heal over time then we become more able to forgive.

The second is that we cannot forgive what we do not understand. Until we have a full understanding of all the damage that was done to us by the abuse, we cannot fully forgive those who abused us. This means at the very least that forgiveness is progressive. I have tried to forgive my father many times for the abuse he inflicted on me, but even now after lots of healing and therapy, there are moments when I realise that something I struggle with in my character or behaviour is actually rooted in the things he did, and I find myself having to forgive him all over again. As I am writing this, I remember something that happened only this week. I am chronically early for every appointment, and tend to get quite anxious if I don't allow quite ridiculous amounts of spare time. This week a friend was taking me to a medical appointment and got quite irritated that I was trying to insist we should set off far earlier than needed. As I thought about it later, I realised that my father would fly into an absolute rage if I was ever late (which in his terms meant not being early) for anything, and he would scream abuse and physically hurt me. On more than one occasion I remember being convinced he was actually going to kill me, because I was running close to the time we had to leave for an appointment. Remembering this, and recognising the impact it still has on me and others, makes me angry with him all over again. Have I forgiven him? I have certainly done my best to do so, but I think the only honest answer is that I am still in the process of forgiving him.

Thirdly, forgiveness does not mean we have to put up with being further abused or intimidated, or that we don't deserve to be protected. I once worked as a therapist with someone who had been abused as a child, who had also gone on to find herself in two abusive marriages. As a result of the therapy she found the courage to leave her second husband, who was still emotionally and physically abusing her. However, he was still part of the same church. She went to the leadership of that church and told them that she didn't feel safe being in church meetings where he was present. She was told by the leaders that she had to forgive him, and that they would not ask him to find another church to attend. Not surprisingly she concluded that they were more interested in supporting her abuser than they were in protecting and looking after her – a situation that almost exactly mirrored the abuse she suffered as a child, when she told her mother that her father was molesting her and her mother chose not to believe her or do anything about it.

All of these three things point to the same basic truths about forgiveness. It is undoubtedly an important part of our journey of healing and recovery that we embrace the need to forgive those who have abused us, but it is not the place we need to start. In fact, it may be a place that we are only able to come to after quite a long time and after our hearts have received considerable healing.

Prayer is not a shortcut

A client comes for her therapy session in deep distress. We have been working through her experience of being physically and emotionally abused as a child more or less from birth onwards. It is something that has caused her significant difficulties in her relationships with others throughout her life.

Today she comes in very quiet, and makes only monosyllabic answers to the questions I ask. When I comment, she says she is worried that she must be a very bad person. I try to reassure her that the abuse didn't happen because she was bad, but she stops me. That isn't what she means. She tells me that she was prayed for at church for God to heal her mental health difficulties. 'They spent hours with me,' she says. 'They prayed into all sorts of strongholds and broke all sorts of spiritual oppression off me, and I did feel better for a day or so, but now I feel just the same as I did before. I was so upset I emailed the pastor, and he told me that if the prayer hadn't worked it must be because I must be coming into agreement with something the enemy was doing.'

I take a deep breath, trying not to show the frustration I feel that some of the good work we have been doing has been undone by a few thoughtless and ignorant words from someone in a position of authority.

Personally speaking, I believe in the power of prayer, and I believe in God's ability to heal. I have seen God at work in people's lives in ways that can only be described as miraculous. However, I do not believe that it is helpful for us to view prayer or any kind of inner-healing ministry as a way of cutting short the process of healing for survivors of childhood abuse. In reality there are no shortcuts. I really wish there were, but all of my experience both as a survivor and as a therapist tells me that the journey of recovery and becoming whole tends to be a long and sometimes complicated one.

Unlike the healing of a physical injury, the healing of injuries to our mind requires our active involvement and cooperation. There are things we need to learn on the journey that cannot be learned any other way. Recovery from the trauma of child abuse is as much about learning how to embrace and transform our pain and distress as it is about getting rid of it. It is as much about learning how to live as a whole person as it is about fixing the brokenness.

We also need to be wary about over-spiritualising something that is primarily a psychological issue. I frequently see survivors who tell me that they have received deliverance or inner-healing prayer to break off a 'spirit of fear', a 'spirit of anger' or even a 'spirit of depression', only to be disappointed a few days, weeks or months later to find that those feelings are still present. There is a reason the feelings are still there. When we were abused we felt afraid, we felt angry, we felt sad, we felt shame. But we had no way of making sense of those feelings or any safe way of discharging them. They remained inside us as psychological filters colouring the way we view ourselves and our lives. Those distressing feelings we experience now are a natural consequence of the awful things that happened to us. Spiritual forces may be able to exploit and amplify those feelings, but they do not cause them. Deliverance or inner-healing ministry can be helpful and can at times bring some relief. There may also be occasions when God brings more permanent freedom. However, this seems to be the exception. Generally speaking, no amount of binding, loosing, rebuking and breaking off is going to address the underlying reasons why we continue to feel afraid, angry, sad and ashamed.

Even if there are spiritual forces at work – and as we have already said we don't actually need to think in terms of 'unclean spirits' to explain our pain and distress, until we are able to deal with our underlying trauma, any spirit that does want to come and exploit our pain is going to find a resting place all ready for it to inhabit.

Prayer is powerful and effective, but it is only a part of the story. Neither prayer nor deliverance nor inner-healing ministry is a magic wand that can somehow be waved over survivors to give them an instant fix. The long-term effects of abuse mean that survivors need those who are willing to walk alongside them, through their pain and distress, rather than looking for a miraculous helicopter to carry them away from it. Prayer is vital and inner-healing ministry can be helpful. However, they are one element of the journey of recovery, rather than the whole story.

Psychology isn't of the devil

When I was a new Christian I found myself in conversation with some people from the church. They asked me what I did for a living, and I told them I was a psychotherapist. There was an awkward silence for a few moments, before one of them said, 'Well, of course, you have Jesus now, so you won't need all that psychology any more.'

I was a bit taken aback to say the least. Was there something wrong with my chosen profession? Did God maybe not like it? I did some asking around, and discovered that there were quite a few people who shared the view that psychotherapy, and in fact any profession related to psychology and mental health, was if not actually wrong, at least perhaps 'not God's best'. The clear implication was that God was our healer, so we did not need to rely on ideas and philosophies that were at best human in origin. I didn't know any different, so I actually stopped practising for a number of years in order to pursue the Lord in other ways.

It wouldn't be fair to suggest that this attitude represents a majority view in the Church, because it certainly doesn't. However, there is a fairly sizeable section of the body of Christ that would hold to this view or something very like it. I have had more than one survivor of abuse tell me that they have been told by ministers and lay people alike that by taking psychiatric medication or by receiving psychotherapy they are displaying a lack of faith in Christ, and that this is the reason they are not yet healed. I have even had clients who were survivors tell me that they have been told that unless they 'repent' of such things and give them up, they will bring God's curse on themselves.

Such attitudes, even the softer, faintly disapproving versions, can be highly destructive to survivors. There is a danger that they could reinforce the belief held by many survivors that there is something wrong with us because we struggle or face challenges. Most of us were told as children that what happened was our fault in some way.

Some of us were even told that the abuse was a judgement from God because of our wickedness. It is imperative that when dealing with survivors, churches do not say or do anything that might seem to confirm those false beliefs.

At the harsher end are views that are in themselves abusive. They represent a form of control, deception and manipulation that can only be called spiritual abuse. But even at the softer end there is something dangerously ignorant about such ideas. It isn't even as if they are necessarily consistent with other beliefs held by those expressing them.

The vast majority of people who are so suspicious of any psychologically based help for survivors of abuse (or indeed for anyone facing any form of mental distress) would not even think about suggesting that someone with a physical illness or injury should not see a doctor or get medical treatment. Most of them would see no conflict between faith in God to heal and the idea that at times God intervenes by guiding the medical professionals to give the right treatments. This, of course, begs the question of why it is that many Christians are able to trust that God is guiding the surgeon's hands, but are not able to trust that God is guiding the psychotherapist's interventions.

As we have already seen, the trauma arising from childhood abuse is both distressing and complex. Without the right help, those of us who have experienced such things are likely to develop ever more severe psychological and emotional difficulties – some to the point where our physical well-being and even our lives are at risk from our own self-destructive actions.

I don't believe that psychotherapy or other psychological interventions have all the answers for survivors. I don't know of many therapists or other helping professionals who do. There is an important role for faith to play in the healing journey of survivors. My personal view is that without our spirituality being a core element in our recovery, we cannot fully break through to the abundant life that Christ offers us. At the same time, we cannot afford to throw the psychological baby out with the bathwater. To do so is a kind of arrogance and spiritual pride that does nothing to glorify God, and is actively destructive to survivors of abuse.

Survivor Resources: Guidance for people praying

Seven things to remember if you want to pray for me

If I am worried about being prayed for, or if my experience of being prayed for has not been a good one, I may find it helpful to print this out and have it handy to show anyone who may want to minister to me.

1. I'm not trying to be awkward.

When I was a child I was abused by adults, and as a result I had a lot of strong feelings I didn't know what to do with. Some of those feelings are still with me, and there are times when, whether I want it to happen or not, I will have a strong emotional reaction to something. Try to remember that if I cry, or run away, or have an angry outburst, or freeze and become mute, I'm not trying to be awkward or difficult. Most of the time I don't even know what has set me off. I'm just expressing my pain and distress and trying to keep myself safe in the only ways I know how.

2. Please ask my permission.

When I was abused as a child, grown-ups did or said horrible things to me without me having any say or any control over it. Please don't assume that it is OK for you simply to come and pray for me without asking permission. If I am going to feel safe with you, I need to know that I have the option to say no. I'm not rejecting you or the help you are offering; I am simply doing my best to feel safe and in control of my surroundings.

3. Don't crowd me.

When I was abused I was little, and adults sometimes stood over me and came into my personal space. If you come too close, and especially if there is more than one of you, particularly if I am sitting, kneeling or lying down, it can feel very threatening. Most of the time I know you are a safe person, but in that situation I can forget and react as if you are not.

4. Be careful about laying hands on me.

Please remember that physical touch doesn't necessarily feel very safe for me. I may associate it with being punished, hurt or molested. Always, always ask my permission before touching me, even if it is just to put a hand on my shoulder. You may know you are a safe person, but when I am in a state of distress, I will not always know or remember that.

5. Don't shout.

Loud voices can be very scary for me. The grown-ups who hurt me when I was a child often had loud voices, and so I may associate shouting or talking loudly with being hurt in some way. Please keep your voice soft and gentle. It will help me to learn to trust you, and to trust the things you are praying over me.

6. Don't ask me to forgive before I'm ready.

Even though I may want to forgive those who abused me, if I am in distress or pain I am almost certainly not ready to do so in any meaningful way. I may not even fully understand yet what I am forgiving them for. Getting to a place where I can understand exactly the ways in which I was hurt by those who abused me or failed to protect me is going to take a while. I know I have been forgiven much, and sooner or later I hope I can forgive in the same way, but please let me choose when I am ready.

7. Don't assume I'm demonised.

Sometimes I get scared, angry or sad. Sometimes I may behave as if I am younger than I really am. None of this means that I am demonised. It is simply that the hurt child inside me is making its feelings known. What that hurt child needs is love, understanding and care. If you try to do deliverance ministry on me when I am in that state, you will be causing further damage to a part of me that is already hurt and broken.

Supporter's Pause for Thought: Who do you say I am?

Jesus asks the question of the disciples, 'Who do you say I am?' and when Peter correctly identifies him as 'the Son of the living God', Jesus tells him that this knowledge could only have come from God (Matthew 16:15-17). Later, in the parable of the sheep and the goats, Jesus says:

> Then the King will say to those on his right, 'Come, you who are blessed by my Father; take your inheritance, the kingdom prepared for you since the creation of the world. For I was hungry and you gave me something to eat, I was thirsty and you gave me something to drink, I was a stranger and you invited me in, I needed clothes and you clothed me, I was ill and you looked after me, I was in prison and you came to visit me.'
>
> Then the righteous will answer him, 'Lord, when did we see you hungry and feed you, or thirsty and give you something to drink? When did we see you a stranger and invite you in, or needing clothes and clothe you? When did we see you ill or in prison and go to visit you?'
>
> The King will reply, 'Truly I tell you, whatever you did for one of the least of these brothers and sisters of mine, you did for me.'
>
> *Matthew 25:34-40*

It is a matter of utmost concern to Jesus that those who follow Him recognise Him not only as God the Son, but also in the disguise of the broken and the marginalised. If we only see one and not the other, we have an incomplete understanding of who He is.

Many survivors have a distorted sense of their own identity, and it is easy for those who encounter them to be taken in by their brokenness and pain, and to believe that this is who they are. Perhaps as a starting point when thinking how to pray for survivors, you could ask yourself the following questions:

- Are you able to recognise in your own discomfort, when dealing with those who were abused as children, an echo of Jesus' question, 'Who do you say I am?'
- Who does God say they are?
- Are you able to recognise the beloved child of God inside all the brokenness and pain?
- How can you remind them when they may have forgotten?

Chapter Four
Your Mind on Trauma

Living on the edge of chaos

I am seeing a woman in her early thirties to assess whether she is suitable for psychotherapy. Everything about her – the way she is dressed, the way she is made up, her whole demeanour – seems to be saying, 'I'm all together.' But I know she must have come to see me for a reason, and there is something about the way she presents that seems brittle and paper-thin. A few questions, and a very different picture begins to emerge. Every day is a battle with feelings of self-loathing, and the urge to harm herself or worse. She describes a perfect childhood that was suddenly shattered when her parents split up, and her mother began seeing a series of men who also sexually abused her.

Abruptly the front crumbles, and she slides off the couch and curls herself into a ball on the floor. She is hyperventilating, and quite literally howling like a wounded animal. I try to talk with her, but she is locked into the chaos of her own experience, unable to respond or to communicate anything more than that she is consumed by indescribable emotional pain. I have seen this many times before, but it is still quite disturbing, and there is always the fear that if something doesn't change, this person might just drop off the edge, overwhelmed by her internal chaos. I move to sit beside her, and ask permission to place a hand on her shoulder. She doesn't object, so rather tentatively I do so and am relieved that it doesn't seem to bother her. I begin to reassure her that she is safe and that no one will hurt her. She is breathing fast and shallowly like a wounded animal. I tell her that I am going to breathe for her, and I start to do a breathing exercise that I know will help to slow everything down and activate the calming chemicals in the brain. As I breathe, I gently squeeze my hand on her shoulder and then release it in the same rhythm. After a few minutes her breathing begins to slow and deepen, and after a while she falls into the same rhythm. She is able to take a step back from the cliff edge of chaos, and become present in the room once again.

As survivors of abuse, many of us live daily on the edge of chaos. It is as if we have one foot on solid ground, and at the same time we can never be sure when that solid ground will crumble away from beneath us. This is because the injury done to our minds – our thoughts, feelings and sense of identity – is so great that at any moment we may encounter something that presses where it hurts. Any reminder of past pain and distress can trigger us into feeling as if the same things are still happening now.

Being triggered in this way is one of the most overwhelming experiences we can have. It is outside our control, automatic, and frequently feels unstoppable. There can be a great sense of shame when out of the blue we suddenly lose control of our emotions, our body, our thought processes. For so long we were placed in situations where we had no power, no control, no agency in our own lives. Those things were taken from us by the people who abused us. Now, at the least provocation it feels just as if it is happening all over again.

For so many of us, some of the emotions and even some of the facts are blurred, hard to recall or even blotted out altogether. All that remains for us is the visceral feeling deep in our core that says: *I am not safe. The terrible things that happened are happening again, and there is nothing I can do to stop it.*

But this is not the truth. Even though it feels like the truth. Even though it feels like the reality we live with sometimes every day, sometimes many times a day. Nevertheless, it is not the truth. No matter how much it used to be a part of our lives, it is no longer a reflection of our current reality. Something dreadful really did happen to us and there was no one then who was able or willing to rescue us. Perhaps it happened just the once, or perhaps it happened many times over. Perhaps there was one single abuser or perhaps there were many. We can't deny the reality, even though for many of us we would love to be able to do just that. Maybe we have even tried hard to forget, to deny, to disconnect from a story that our dread and panic tells us cannot have a good ending. But deep down somewhere, we know that these things happened, even if we can't remember exactly what they were, even if we try to minimise it. However, that is where the truth stops, because for most of us it isn't happening now. The awful things that happened are over, even if their effect lingers on, even if we are still living wounded and scarred by what was done to us.

It isn't happening now, but when we are triggered all that rational knowledge and reasoning goes right out of the window. It's as if that part of our mind goes completely offline, and the dreadful waves of panic are let loose to sweep through our bodies and minds over and over and over, until we think we might be swept away by the force of it and never find our feet again.

It is at this point, when we are triggered and overwhelmed by the memories and feelings, that we most need to feel our feet upon the ground. We need to be able to touch the bottom and know that we cannot sink any further. We need to know that there is something solid we can stand on so that when the waves of panic and pain and distress recede, they won't sweep us away with them into a past we can barely dare to think about. This is when we really need to know that there is a place where we can find our ground. There is a place where we can stand in the storm. There is a place that can hold us safe. More than this, we need to know where we can find it. We need to know just *how* we can ground ourselves, most especially when there is no one there to help us.

When we come right down to it, the things that can help us are not big. They are the very little and simple things: movement, sensory input, the simple rhythms of breathing in and out. The things listed in the next section may not seem like much, but they are our lifeline. Perhaps they will only make a little difference, but as we keep doing them, as we keep working our way down the sections from top to bottom, gradually things will change.

Instead of feeling paralysed by fear, we discover we can move just a little – perhaps it's only the end of a finger to begin with, but we can build on that. Instead of having our minds flooded with the awful images, sounds, smells and sensations, we discover that we can choose to focus our attention on something different. We can choose to fill our minds with something that is not toxic or dangerous to us, even if it's only for a few seconds at first. The more we do that, the longer we can keep our minds free of those things that are no longer our present reality.

Instead of feeling unable to catch our breath, we discover that little by little we can begin to slow our breathing down, to even out the rhythm, so it is less jerky and becomes more even. We discover too, that as we slow it down, our heartbeat slows towards a normal rate as well. We stop sweating quite so much, stop feeling quite so sick, and eventually everything in our body starts to find a resting place.

Perhaps then, when we are a little calmer, we can pick up the phone, and call or text someone who cares about us. We can reach out to someone safe who will respond with care and love, and we can finally know ourselves standing once more on solid ground.

The chaos is not random

Like everyone else, survivors have good days and bad days. However, our bad days tend to be darker and to persist for longer, and our good days tend to be less solid and enduring. Our day-to-day experience can at times be quite hard to navigate. Sometimes it seems as if life is full of minefields, obstacles and pitfalls. At any moment we can find ourselves tripping over things we didn't expect. On good days life can feel like sailing across a calm sea. On bad days it can feel like we went for a swim in the local pool only to find a force eleven gale whipping the water up into twenty-foot waves that threaten to overwhelm and drown us.

When we are in the middle of that kind of chaos and uncertainty, it can be really useful to know that what we are experiencing is not random. It has an explanation, and though we may struggle to grasp exactly what it is, it does have meaning. There are reasons for our internal chaos and there are ways to navigate it safely.

In this chapter we are going to look at those somewhat chaotic experiences, and discover the reasons why they happen. We are also going to look at some ways we can begin to steer our way through them and find ourselves in calmer waters. If we are in the middle of the storm right now, we really need the reassurance that despite how things feel, there is a way through this. That's the good news. The rest of the news isn't bad exactly, but it may be a bit less easy for us to hear. It is simply this: *yes, there is a way through, but there isn't a way around.* There aren't any quick fixes, and there aren't any shortcuts, but there are plenty of ways in which we can build resilience, and learn to navigate our way through even the worst storms.

What trauma does to your brain

When we are abused or traumatised, particularly when we are young, it has a set of very specific effects on our brains. Those effects may vary in how severe or complex they are, but they are fairly well-known these days, and if we had the right scanning equipment we could actually measure or even show images of the long-term effects of trauma on the brain. This isn't a textbook on neurobiology, so I'm not going to go into huge detail, but it is probably helpful for us to have an understanding of the broad picture of what is going on in our brains, because that affects what happens in our bodies and our minds (mind not being the same thing as brain). This in turn can help us to understand better what is going on in our daily experience as we try to navigate some of the storms in our lives.

We should probably talk about what trauma does to our *brains*, because structurally we don't just have one brain. We have a number of different brains that are linked, and in an ideal world all of them work together. These different brains develop at different rates, and reflect the various stages of development that a child goes through. Most of us are probably aware that the brain is divided into two halves or hemispheres: the logical, rational, verbal left brain, and the visual, creative, non-linear right brain. But our brains are divided into back, middle and front brain as well.

The back brain is the oldest, in that it develops first. It governs some of our most basic instincts, particularly in the face of danger or threat. The back brain is focused on survival and getting its needs met. In the face of danger it is the back brain that makes a snap decision about whether we fight or flee or freeze. Sometimes this back brain is known as the *reptilian brain*, because it has about the same level of development and range of responses as the average reptile.

The mid-brain develops next and, among other functions, this is where we store and process the memories and feelings we have about our experiences, whether positive or negative. This part of the brain is technically called the *limbic system*, and is sometimes known as the *mammalian brain*, because it functions at a developmental level common to most mammals. As well as storing and processing memories, this mid-brain also has a part to play in how we relate to others. In terms of human survival, it is where the decisions about who to bond with and relate to in order to ensure that we are protected and cared for are made.

The front brain or *neocortex* develops last. It is where, among other things, we do most of our conscious thinking and decision-making. This is the part of the brain that allows us to think in symbolic and abstract ways. So much of our language and understanding of the world outside us is rooted here.

There are also certain parts of the brain whose function is essentially to communicate with the other parts of the brain, and generally to make the whole thing work together in a healthy and appropriate way.

Of course, this is a highly simplified picture. But you get the general idea. The natural functions of the brain are split up among its various parts, but ideally they cooperate and work together as one. Unsurprisingly, the mind – our patterns of thinking, feeling and relating – mirrors the basic *separate but working-together* structure of the brain. However, what happens when something disrupts that normal functioning and the communication between the different parts of both our brain and our mind?

Trauma of any kind causes our back brain to go into overdrive, preparing to meet the threat by getting ready to run away, fight back or freeze like a rabbit in the headlights. Our body is flooded with stress hormones – adrenaline, cortisol and others. As a result, our front brain shuts down and basically goes offline for anything between thirty minutes and a few hours. Our mid-brain doesn't exactly shut down, but it starts to operate in a different way. We may become flooded with memories and feelings as the mid-brain tries to make sense of what is happening *now* in terms of what we have experienced before. To put it another way, once the immediate 'fight, flight, freeze' response of the back brain begins to dial down, we can find ourselves troubled by intrusive memories, images, thoughts and feelings, usually negative and often related to other traumatic experiences. This can be incredibly scary, painful and distressing to us. If we are abused repeatedly or over a long period of time, our mind can become stuck in these patterns, so it becomes easier for us to respond to all sorts of challenges by feeling intense fear, pain and other forms of distress.

Those responses of fear, pain and distress are completely understandable and appropriate under the circumstances. In their way they can even be helpful – what psychologists call *adaptive*, because these are the responses that caused our ancestors to run away from some animal in the forest that wanted to eat them, or that cause caregivers to pick up a distressed baby to attend to their needs and comfort them. However, the problem is that if we are *too* overwhelmed with fear, pain and distress, or if it happens too often, our mind goes on high alert, even in response to events or people that don't necessarily present a threat. So instead of being able to function in everyday life, we may at any time, for reasons we don't fully understand, become paralysed or want to run away, or have an aggressive outburst. In effect we are responding to a danger that for the most part isn't actually real any more.

It is important that we understand that this isn't a mistake or a design flaw. Our brains were actually designed to work this way when faced with overwhelming threat, because this sort of compartmentalising of the different functions of the brain when we were too small to defend ourselves against those who abused us actually gave us the best chance of surviving, both physically and psychologically. It is a mechanism that is known as *dissociation*, meaning a disconnection between the different parts of the brain or the different functions of the mind. We are going to be talking about dissociation a fair bit, as we try to understand more about why we respond the way we do to things, and how we can learn to navigate the challenges of life more effectively.

The experience of dissociation

Perhaps the first thing to say is that dissociation is a totally normal function of the human mind. It is one of the ways we learn to deal with stress and discomfort. Everyone experiences dissociation from time to time, just in the normal course of life. Most of us have had the experience of driving to a familiar place, perhaps when we are feeling a bit tired or under a bit of stress. We arrive at our destination, or at a particular point along the way, and realise that we have absolutely no memory of having actually driven there. We remember setting off, and possibly the first part of the journey, but now we have got here, and we can remember very little or even nothing. Nevertheless, we must have navigated the traffic, dealt with road junctions and roundabouts, possibly even stopped to let people use a zebra crossing; we just can't remember any of it. It can be a really disconcerting experience. The lack of damage to the car and the lack of flashing blue lights chasing us means that presumably we made the drive reasonably safely, but not being able to remember it leaves us with a certain nagging doubt.

This experience is sometimes known as motorway amnesia or highway hypnosis. It is in fact an example of dissociation at work in everyday life. Of course, this form of dissociation isn't necessarily linked to trauma, but it does show us what the mind is capable of doing to protect us from even everyday stress, under the right circumstances. That defensive mechanism is incredibly useful to us, especially when we are children, and the world can present us with many unfamiliar challenges, some of which may be frightening, distressing or painful.

If we think about the example we used earlier of a small child who is frightened by a noisy dog, we can see how dissociation is helpful in helping the child not be overwhelmed by the scary experience. The child is scared of the dog, and their body and developing mind are flooded with stress hormones, to the point where it begins to feel overwhelming. The child cries and screams, and they begin to struggle to breathe. Suddenly, it is as if the child can see themselves down the wrong end of a telescope, or as if they were slightly not in their body. The sound of the dog barking and the visual images of the dog jumping up are still there, but muted and experienced as if at a distance. Even though they can see themselves still reacting with fear and distress, it is as if it isn't really happening to them. There is a crying child they are watching reacting to the dog, and then there is the child who is watching the crying child reacting. The effect on the body is that the breathing begins to regulate and become even again, and before long the neurochemicals that reduce the stress reaction begin to flood through the child's body, allowing them to calm a little. Then, just as suddenly as it started, the dissociative episode is over. There is just one child dealing with the aftermath of their scary experience, perhaps still crying a little, but nowhere near as distressed as they were.

Again, this is a normal experience of dissociation, a relatively common reaction to unusually stressful situations. People who have been in or near serious car accidents report a similar phenomenon. Time seems to slow down, sounds become muted, and they find they can watch their bodies reacting almost calmly to the situation, as if they were looking at themselves from outside. I remember one occasion when I was driving along the motorway with my wife and her mother, and I saw a car ahead of us begin to weave a bit between lanes. I can remember thinking, *that driver isn't alright,* and then watching as the car swerved onto the hard shoulder, and then back across all three lanes ahead of us and into the path of a van. I can remember telling my passengers to hold on, and then it was exactly as if time had slowed to a crawl. I saw the car get hit by the van and spun around into the path of a lorry, while the van that had hit the car went crashing into the central reservation. The car was hit by the lorry and came hurtling across our path, clipping another vehicle as it did so. As if in slow motion I saw my hands on the steering wheel and the gear stick, moving of their own accord without any conscious direction on my part. Without knowing how I did it, I managed to steer a path between the various vehicles and bits of debris, and found myself the other side of what was now a multivehicle accident. Still calm, I pulled over onto the hard shoulder and called the emergency services. Then and only then did I start to shake.

The spectrum of dissociation

The experience of dissociation is best thought of as existing on some sort of spectrum or continuum.

At one end are the normal everyday experiences of dissociation that all of us can experience whether we have a history of abuse or other trauma or not. Slightly further along the spectrum are dissociative experiences that can be thought of as normal responses to an abnormal situation. My experience of narrowly avoiding a multivehicle pile-up would probably fall into this category.

Further along the spectrum of dissociation, we come to experiences that are still quite common but which are reactions to events that are definitely traumatic. These reactions that we call *post-traumatic* can seem slightly crazy to someone who doesn't understand that they are in fact a fairly desperate attempt by the mind to protect us from being overwhelmed by the abusive or traumatic experiences we've had.

At the other end of the spectrum are a group of dissociative experiences that are rather less common.

These tend to be grouped under the term *dissociative disorders* by psychiatrists, though personally I believe that the *disorder* tag is both unhelpful and untrue. As we shall see, what these experiences at the far end of the dissociative spectrum actually represent are highly intelligent ways in which the mind is trying to protect us from the overwhelming pain and distress connected to the abuse we suffered. In effect it is helping us to stay functional in the face of our struggles.

PTSD

The term post-traumatic stress disorder, or PTSD, has pretty much entered the common understanding of most people. There has been a fair bit of coverage of the difficulties faced by service people returning from combat zones. In fact a great deal of the early work to identify and understand PTSD was carried out with veterans returning from the Vietnam war in the 1960s and 1970s, as described by Bessel van der Kolk.[13] It was realised that people who had traumatic experiences while serving in the military tended to have a particular set of responses that were no longer *adaptive* responses to trauma, but were instead *maladaptive*, and causing problems for them in their lives.

PTSD isn't limited to combat veterans, though. Most of us who were abused as children will experience some sort of post-traumatic responses to what happened to us, and many will develop the long-lasting and very distressing condition that is known as PTSD.

---

[13] Bessel van der Kolk, *The Body Keeps the Score* (London: Penguin, 2015).

Generally speaking, there are three specific things that characterise PTSD. Usually all three are present, though different people may experience them at different levels.

Being triggered

When we experience a post-traumatic reaction, or if we develop the long-term version that is known as PTSD, one of the most common things we are likely to experience is what is known as *re-experiencing*, though more colloquially we would probably refer to it as *being triggered*. Being triggered can be incredibly distressing to us. Essentially what happens is that something that may be apparently innocuous (the trigger) sets off a sudden recall of traumatic experiences in a way that can be highly disturbing and overwhelming.

This sudden recollection can cover pretty much the whole range of experiences that we have had relating to the abuse we suffered.

Emotional reactions: Sometimes we may become flooded with strong feelings. We may react with sudden anger, fear, sadness or shame, in a way that seems out of proportion to what is actually happening at the time. The likelihood is that these are dissociated feelings and reactions. Perhaps they are appropriate to the abuse we experienced, but for whatever reason, we weren't able to allow ourselves to feel or express them at the time. Now, in response to the trigger, and perhaps because we are in a safer (though not necessarily ideal) situation, our mind reconnects with our feelings and responses.

Disturbances in perception: We can also find ourselves flooded with all sorts of perceptions, by which we mean sights, sounds, physical sensations, smells or tastes, that do not reflect what is actually going on at the time. Usually these will be of things that happened at the time of the abuse. They are often known as *flashbacks*, and they can be incredibly distressing to survivors of abuse. Sometimes we may also experience flashbacks as dreams, in which abuse is either re-experienced or is symbolically re-enacted.

Flashbacks may vary in intensity. At the lower level they come in the form of intrusive images and thoughts – sometimes known as *snapshot memories*. At the top end of the scale, we can feel as if the traumatic experiences are still happening, and we find ourselves reacting in exactly the same way as we did (or possibly as we wish we had been able to) at the time.

I remember once doing some training on trauma with a small group of people. There came a point when I was talking about something that must have been a trigger for one of the participants, because she abruptly ran from the room and was found in the corner of the kitchen in a foetal curl, rocking and crying. When we were finally able to coax her out of the state she was in, she reported that she had felt very young, and that she was convinced she was about to be sexually assaulted by the group of adults in the training room. Later work with this person revealed that this had in fact been her experience as a child, and that the corner of the kitchen was often where she would go to hide afterwards to comfort herself.

Physical reactions: Sometimes survivors, in response to a trigger, will begin to manifest some of the physical responses to trauma. These are sometimes known as *body memories*. These can take place alongside or overlapping with flashbacks, but they can also happen when there are no other apparent perceptual disturbances.

Body memories can include all sorts of things. Most commonly, we find ourselves sweating, have trouble breathing, or our heartbeat races. However, we can also feel nauseous, be sick, or even wet or soil ourselves with fear. Sometimes we may experience psychosomatic pain or other physical sensations related to what happened to us.

These physical reactions, again, are often incredibly distressing for survivors. There is something that feels particularly invasive and out of control about having our body react in an unpleasant way, and the nature of some of the reactions can also cause us a considerable degree of shame.

Recovered memories: We need to understand that re-experiencing can sometimes represent the recovery of dissociated memories. This is something of a controversial topic, and even today with much evidence to the contrary, there are still psychiatrists who do not believe that it is possible for memories of trauma to be dissociated and therefore not consciously remembered. However, the dissociation of traumatic memories is actually quite common among survivors of child abuse. These are memories that would have been too overwhelming and distressing for us to have been consciously aware of as children. Therefore the mind, being resourceful, uses its dissociative mechanisms to push those memories into the unconscious, where they remain either not known or only partially known, until we are old enough and resilient enough to begin to remember and process what happened to us.

My own experience was that I always remembered the abuse I experienced by a piano teacher from the age of eleven onwards. However, it was only when I began to work through those experiences with a therapist in my twenties that I began to have dreams and flashbacks about being abused by my father and others at a much younger age.

Very often it is the content of flashbacks and body memories that are the first steps towards recovering these dissociated memories, which is often a very important part of our journey of recovery and healing.

Hyperarousal

The second core feature of PTSD is what is called *hyperarousal* or sometimes *hypervigilance*. Hyperarousal means that we can be highly reactive. It can manifest in a number of ways. Survivors tend to be easily startled, and sometimes we may seem quite jumpy, edgy or nervous, especially if what is known as our *startle reflex* is triggered.

We also tend to be constantly checking our surroundings. This is especially the case when the abuse we suffered involved something unexpected happening or unpredictable behaviour from others. This hypervigilant checking of our surroundings is usually our unconscious attempt to prepare ourselves for the unexpected. Human beings tend to be characterised by their ability to recognise patterns, and many survivors of childhood abuse take this pattern recognition ability to a new level. We very often notice things that others don't seem to be aware of. We see when something is out of its usual place or out of schedule. This is because anything that deviates from what is expected may be a potential threat.

Hyperarousal also affects our sleep patterns. Very often those who have been abused as children will have disrupted sleep. Sometimes we don't get much sleep at all, or if we do, we may sleep very fitfully. At other times we may prefer to sleep at times when our mind tells us it is likely to be safer. For example, we might sleep only a few hours a night during the week, and wake often in quite an alert state, but at the weekends when we are able to sleep in late, we catch up on our missed sleep, often during more daylight hours.

This hypervigilance is often a completely unconscious process. For example, we may not realise why we always take a seat in a café facing the door, or why in a cinema we always choose to sit on the end of the row. In fact, we are always unconsciously trying to prepare ourselves for whatever threat might come through the door, or to make sure we have an easy escape route.

When I was first married, my wife would sometimes get cross because in social settings I tended to find it hard to focus exclusively on the person I was talking to. Instead my eyes would be constantly roving around the room, and I would be checking in to some of the other conversations going on around me. I knew it wasn't a lack of listening skills – for a psychotherapist that would be a fatal flaw – but clearly something was going on. It took a while to realise that because as a child I had experienced some significant trauma that took place at adult parties, I was being hypervigilant and checking my surroundings to see who in the room presented a danger to me.

Hyperarousal may best be thought of as one of the ways in which the mind attempts to manage its environment to avoid being triggered. Survivors of trauma tend to view the world through an unconscious filter that frames it as a hostile and dangerous place. As such, survivors of abuse often have little choice but to be hypervigilant in order to feel safe and in control, at least to a degree.

Avoidance

The third core feature of PTSD is known as *avoidance*. Again, it is probably helpful to remember that avoidance is an unconscious strategy, and like hypervigilance is a way of controlling and managing the effects of the trauma that comes from our being abused as children. The chances are that we will not be aware that we are engaging in avoidant behaviour. If we are aware, we almost certainly will not realise why, at least until we are able to make the connection.

Avoidance can include a whole range of things. Most commonly it will include our staying away from the places and people that our minds associate with the abuse, even if that association is mistaken. This may sometimes lead to us staying away from previously enjoyed activities.

A former colleague of mine once worked with an ex-soldier who had served in Northern Ireland at the height of the Troubles. When he returned to civilian life he developed a number of the symptoms of PTSD. Among these was the fact that on his way to and from work he would drive about fifteen miles out of his way, and avoided using the most direct and obvious route. On further investigation, it was discovered that the most obvious route took him past a particular configuration of streets in which he had to drive past the end of a short street, at the other end of which was a house with large first-floor windows. It turned out that this was exactly the same configuration of streets and the same style of house he and his patrol had been driving past in Northern Ireland when they came under sniper fire, and three of the patrol were killed.

Sometimes we can develop a very numbing form of depression that insulates us from everyday life, and any possible contact with triggers. At other times we may develop severe anxiety, which again prevents us from doing things that might bring us into contact with possible triggers. Some of us detach ourselves emotionally, as the mind decides that it is safer not to feel the difficult emotions associated with the abuse. Sometimes we can develop quite an elaborate front, to prevent others from detecting that anything may be wrong.

One survivor I have worked with likes to describe her emotional detachment as a 'concrete fort' and pretends that there is nothing going on under the surface, despite the fact that her avoidant defences are actually quite brittle, and can suddenly collapse, revealing the depth of the struggle underneath.

Some survivors experience a form of perceptual detachment, which is actually another way the mind dissociates from difficult experiences. This comes in two forms. The first is known as *depersonalisation* – the perception that they themselves, or a part of them, is not quite real. The second is known as *derealisation* – the perception that the rest of the world is not quite real.

Another form of avoidance has to do with what can sometimes happen to our memories of what happened to us. It is not at all uncommon for memories of abuse, or at least some aspects of it, to be split off through the mind dissociating. It is a form of selective amnesia that operates to protect us from having to remember experiences that we might find too overwhelming.

Survivor Resources: How to ground myself

When I am triggered I have a *startle reaction*. I may even have a panic attack. Sometimes I freeze – I feel like I can't move, think or speak. When this happens, these are ways I can ground myself and bring myself back from being triggered.

Start at the top of the list and work your way SLOWLY down the different sections…

MOVE my body
- In small ways to start with, gradually becoming bigger
- One limb at a time – eg first a finger, then a hand, then an arm
- Stand up straight
- Stretch out limbs
- Walk around a little

FOCUS on my environment
- What can I see?
- How many circular objects are there? Square objects?
- How many blue objects can I see? How about other colours?
- Name a few objects

- What sounds can I hear?
- Can I hear myself breathing?
- Can I hear cars in the distance?
- Name a few sounds

CHANGE my sensory input
- Have something soft or comforting to touch or stroke (piece of cloth, soft toy, etc). How does it feel against my skin?
- Smell something pleasant (hand cream, piece of orange, etc) – describe the smell to myself
- Taste something nice (chocolate, coffee, etc) – think of a good time when I tasted this before

BREATHE
- Breathe into my tummy – as low down as I can manage
- Breathe slowly – in to the count of three and out to the count of six
- Focus on the sensation of my lungs filling and emptying
- Do this at least ten times (count them on my fingers)
- Repeat until I feel more calm

Supporter's Pause for Thought: How do I respond?

That day when evening came, he said to his disciples, 'Let us go over to the other side.' Leaving the crowd behind, they took him along, just as he was, in the boat. There were also other boats with him. A furious squall came up, and the waves broke over the boat, so that it was nearly swamped. Jesus was in the stern, sleeping on a cushion. The disciples woke him and said to him, 'Teacher, don't you care if we drown?'

He got up, rebuked the wind and said to the waves, 'Quiet! Be still!' Then the wind died down and it was completely calm.

Mark 4:35-39

Sometimes it is hard to know how to pray in the face of emotional turmoil. Remember you do not have to fix anything. Rather you are here to connect with the survivors you are supporting, and to facilitate their encounter with the presence of Christ. Jesus was able to calm the storm, by His presence and His words. This is what love does. It brings calm, order and meaning to what may otherwise feel chaotic and overwhelming.

When you support survivors of abuse you are re-presenting the ministry of Jesus. You are His hands, His feet, His lips. When you speak, your words are His words. When you sit listening or in silent companionship, you embody His presence. When you love, you do so with His heart.

There may be many specific things you can pray for survivors. As you get to know them you will become familiar with the challenges of their lives. But sometimes we just need something simple to pray for those in crisis. Here is a four-part outline for prayer that you can elaborate to put some flesh on the bones and make your own. Pray:

- That they would have a tangible sense of God's unconditional love for them.

- That they would know His peace that passes understanding.

- That they would know themselves held safe and secure by Him.

- That He would protect them from all harm, whether physical, emotional or spiritual.

Chapter Five
The Fractured Soul

Broken-hearted

> The Spirit of the Sovereign LORD is on me,
> because the LORD has anointed me
> to proclaim good news to the poor.
> He has sent me to bind up the broken-hearted,
> to proclaim freedom for the captives
> and release from darkness for the prisoners
> *Isaiah 61:1*

When Jesus reads from the Scriptures in Nazareth, he quotes Isaiah 61 (see Luke 4:16-21), and says that he has come, among other things, to 'bind up the broken-hearted'. That word *broken-hearted* in the original Hebrew that Jesus would have been reading from is *shabar*, which literally means fractured or shattered into pieces in our innermost being. It is a good phrase to describe what happens to us when we have been traumatised by childhood abuse.

I sometimes think of our soul or personality being like a pottery vase, with the abuse that we have experienced being like blows inflicted on the vase, which damage it. In the same way that the vase becomes cracked, broken or even shattered into pieces, so our soul or our personality becomes fractured to a greater or lesser degree by the abuse we have suffered. Almost always our soul will be cracked by the trauma or childhood abuse. Sometimes the damage may be even more profound, with our soul being broken or even shattered into many pieces.

This fracturing is the dissociation caused by abuse that we spoke of in the previous chapter. The reality is that when we have been abused in childhood, and especially when there are a number of complicating factors to the trauma we sustained, we will be fractured to one degree or another. Instead of being a single coherent whole, our soul, our mind or our personality will be dissociated into a number of different parts. Each of these parts is disconnected from the others. Sometimes this is a small disconnection – when the pottery vase is cracked. At other times there may be a larger disconnection, as if one or two pieces were broken off the vase. Occasionally the fracturing and disconnection is more complete, as if the vase were shattered into pieces and fragments.

Our journey of healing and recovery is like taking those cracked and shattered parts of ourselves, and gradually putting them back together again.

In this chapter we are going to explore what it is like for survivors to experience life fractured – with our hearts broken – and begin to understand how those fractured parts of us might be made whole again.

We are not sick

It is important to understand that we are not ill. Perhaps unusually for a mental health professional, I question the language that speaks of mental and emotional distress in terms of disease or illness. These things are not helpful and they are not true for us as survivors. Whether we like it or not there is still a stigma attached to mental illness. Although no one may quite like to say so out loud, it carries connotations of uncleanness and shame. Those who are so afflicted are outcasts from the mainstream of society.

Those of us who have been abused as children already feel ourselves to be unclean. We are often filled with shame. We believe ourselves to be unworthy of inclusion. Anything that reinforces those feelings in us is not going to be of much use to us on our journey of recovery and healing.

The other problem with what is sometimes known as the *disease model*, or *biomedical model* of mental illness, is that it seems to view most types of emotional and psychological distress as being incurable illnesses. These are conditions that we can learn to manage, but we should not hope that we can ever fully recover. When we are living with the turbulent thoughts and feelings that are the long-term legacy of the abuse we suffered, such a view can rob us of our hope. It is as if we are being told that the best we can expect is a managed OK-ness, but a life overflowing with goodness is forever beyond our reach.

Many types of mental distress arising from child abuse are often labelled as incurable illnesses. However, they are in fact nothing of the sort. They are injuries that with the right help and support we can overcome and move on from.

Dissociative disconnection

All survivors dissociate to one degree or another. It is one of our survival mechanisms. Without it, when we were children we would have been completely overwhelmed by the awful things that were happening to us. Dissociation is what helped us to stay functional and kept us relatively sane.

However, no matter how helpful dissociation was to us when we were children, as we grow up the dissociation that used to keep us safe and stable begins to break down and becomes less helpful. This is probably because as we grow up, life becomes more complex. It presents us with challenges that are less obviously threatening than the abuse we suffered, and dissociation doesn't help us cope with these more subtle stresses and strains quite as well. Sooner or later, the way in which dissociation operates is likely to become problematic in itself. The very things that used to help us feel emotionally safe and stable become some of the things that knock us emotionally off balance. This is when we may find ourselves being labelled with some 'mental disorder' or another.

There are a whole range of labels that we could pick up. Some of them are what are known as 'mood disorders' – because most survivors experience some level of depression and anxiety at some point. Sometimes we may be 'diagnosed' with a psychotic disorder, such as schizophrenia or bipolar disorder, because for many survivors our ability to make sense of the difference between what is going on inside our minds and how we perceive external reality is dislocated in some way. Some of us may be labelled with one or more *personality disorders*, which simply means that our personality functions in ways that society views as unacceptable or problematic. There may even be times when, owing to the dissociation that arises from child abuse, we are diagnosed with a learning disability or an organic malfunction of the brain, such as dyslexia or dyspraxia, or perhaps Asperger syndrome or other similar conditions now usually grouped together as autistic spectrum disorder (ASD).

The reality, however, is that for most of us, although we may display the 'symptoms' of these 'disorders', they are actually a by-product of the dissociation that once kept us safe, but which has now stopped working as well or as flexibly as we need it to. The longer I have spent working with survivors of abuse, the more I have come to wonder whether some of the more serious mental health conditions are actually more a case of the abuse survivor's dissociation having broken down in a more profound way, or perhaps never having fully been established in the first place.

I remember working with someone who was subjected to organised abuse of a particularly horrific nature, based within but not confined to the family. She had learned to dissociate to quite an extreme degree, and this capacity had enabled her to remain reasonably functional. Her younger siblings, who had also been subjected to similar types of abuse, were less able to function in everyday life. They were variously diagnosed with a range of psychiatric 'disorders'. It is possible that the siblings simply lacked the same capacity to dissociate, and therefore developed other ways of showing their mental distress. However, it is also possible that the mental health system misinterpreted the signs of dissociation as indicating psychosis or some other 'mental illness'.

All dissociation involves a certain disconnection misalignment in our mental processes. It is this disconnection that may look like mental illness to an outside observer. In addition to the various types of 'mental illness' that we have just mentioned, there is also a group of what are called *dissociative disorders*, all of which show different types and degrees of disconnection between our thoughts, feelings, physical sensations, memory and behaviour. Just to give us a helpful mental picture to work with: if we think about these types of disconnection in terms of mental illness it would be a bit like having a number of different boxes, each with a specific label. Looked at as different levels of disconnection, it is more like a set of concentric circles, so the more common types of disconnection contain the less common ones.

Complex PTSD

Almost all survivors of childhood abuse will have a post-traumatic reaction, and almost all will go on to develop PTSD. Many of us will also fit the criteria for complex PTSD (CPTSD).

What this means in practice is that we show some of the signs of PTSD to quite a high degree, and that we dissociate more easily. However, what really defines our PTSD as being 'complex' is that our experience of abuse has some of the complicating factors that we looked at in Chapter Two.

As a result of this complexity, it is likely that some of the things that are used to help people with PTSD are not going to work quite as effectively on us. The difficulty is that when we try to work through the trauma associated with the abuse, it is likely that this in itself will trigger other memories in us.

This does not mean that we can't be helped. It simply means that it is a bit of a longer journey, with more obstacles along the way.

When we experience CPTSD we become quite disconnected from the reality of what is happening in the present for us. Even though right here and now there is no actual danger, the thoughts, feelings, physical responses and memories of the abuse we suffered are incredibly strong and intrusive. Their intensity disconnects us from our present experience, so that it all feels like it is still happening now. At the same time, the parts of us that remember what happened may be disconnected from the parts of us that feel the emotions about what happened and the parts of us that feel the physical sensation of what happened. All of these are disconnected from the parts of us that want to respond and do something in response to the feelings or the physical sensations or the memories.

What it looks like to someone else is that we have a strong emotional reaction – maybe we run away, have an angry outburst, or start crying. But when someone asks us why we are doing these things, we may not really know. It can look very strange and a bit crazy from the outside, but that is because all these things have become disconnected from each other. If we are able to make the connections and put everything into the context of what happened to us, it all becomes much more understandable.

If we think of our analogy of the fractured vase, complex PTSD is like a vase that has been hit hard enough that it is cracked in a number of places. This makes it very fragile and it doesn't always hold water well. However, the structure of the vase manages to hold together for the most part. There is a danger that with any further jolts or shocks the cracks in the vase may become greater; it is even possible that with another blow the vase might break altogether.

Depersonalisation/Derealisation

Another type of dissociative disconnection happens when our consciousness becomes disconnected from our physical perceptions. Sometimes this means that all or part of our physical body starts to feel unreal to us. Sometimes all or part of our body starts to feel numb, or we may start to feel that in some way it doesn't really belong to us. Sometimes we are even able to tolerate high levels of pain, because we have learned to disconnect from the physical sensations. This is what is known as *depersonalisation.*

I worked with a survivor who, whenever she was triggered by certain things, would go numb, or have the sensation of pins and needles in her body. After a while it became clear that this was connected with an incident in her childhood, in which she was assaulted so badly that she sustained a serious concussion. Although her memory for these events was fragmentary and only came back to her over a period of time, it eventually became clear that

131

the numbness and physical sensations were those she experienced when she lost consciousness, and when she regained consciousness a while later.

Again, this may sound fairly crazy, but if we think about it in the context that our bodies were made to feel things that they didn't want to feel, it makes sense that we learned to dissociate from the physical sensations.

Other effects of depersonalisation are more subtle. When our mind disconnects from the pain and other unpleasant physical sensations that were experienced in childhood, it does so because it is trying to protect us from having to feel what happened. However, this comes at a cost. Those physical sensations that have not been felt often make themselves known later in other ways. This means that we are more likely to develop a whole host of stress-related physical symptoms, from migraines and bad backs to some long-term and serious chronic illnesses.

Sometimes our disconnection is not so much from our physical body, but from the world around us. This can feel as if everything around us is not quite real, perhaps as if we are moving through a fog, or looking at everything down the wrong end of a telescope. When we are in this state of disconnection, which is known as *derealisation*, we can find ourselves looking at familiar objects or even people and not recognising what or who they are. It can be a very strange feeling to look at something or someone familiar, and to know that we should know what or who they are, but not actually to be able to place them or know what our relationship to them is.

Essentially, what is happening is very much the same as what happens with depersonalisation. When we were small and being abused, our mind tried to protect us by disconnecting us from the threat, pain or distress. With derealisation our mind numbed us to an external world that felt too dangerous for us to engage with fully. Having learned to do that when we were small, our mind continues to use the same protective strategies now that we are older, whenever it faces a situation that seems to us as if it could be threatening or distressing in some way.

If we want to think of depersonalisation and derealisation in terms of our image of the fractured vase, it is as if there is a piece of the vase that is broken off from the rest of it. We can replace it and it will generally stay in place, until something happens to jolt the vase again, when it becomes dislodged once more.

These episodes of depersonalisation and derealisation generally don't last very long. They can be anything from a few minutes to a few hours, but eventually, as our sense of being under threat calms down, we begin to reconnect with ourselves or with the world around us.

Borderline personality

There is another type of disconnection that is often known as *borderline personality disorder*, or BPD.

When we were abused as children, and particularly if the abuse started when we were very young – before the age of three – our ability to distinguish between what is real and not real may have been impaired. Even now we are older, our internal sense of reality may be partially disconnected from what is really going on around us. There can also be a disconnection between our emotions and reality, as we flip between responding to what is really happening and what is going on inside us.

There was so much fear around for us when we were children that we were constantly on high alert, waiting to be hurt once again. This led to us trying to predict from the very smallest clues what was going to happen. It became very important for us to be able to guess what sort of emotional state other people were in, so that we could prepare ourselves in case they were going to abuse or mistreat us in some way. We started to attribute meaning to all sorts of things to try to predict what was going to happen. Some of the time our predictions were right, but the rest of the time they were wrong. However, our fear was so great that we weren't really able to distinguish between when they were right or when they were wrong, so we began to respond the same either way. This inability to distinguish between threatening and non-threatening situations leaves us unable to deal with any ambiguity. People and situations seem either wholly good or wholly bad, but we cannot conceive of them being a mixture of the two. This is sometimes known as *black and white thinking*.

The problem with black and white thinking is that it doesn't match the reality, which is that all people have good and not so good traits. Therefore, people with a borderline personality have to alternate between seeing a person or a situation as wholly good or wholly bad. When we do this, our emotional responses also have to change to match how we are viewing things at that moment. Just as there is no ambiguity in the way we perceive things, so there is no ambiguity in the ways we respond. This can lead to us displaying some extremely unstable emotional responses. One time we see our friend and she seems wholly good to us, so we shower her with affirmation and kindness. Another time, because of something quite minor that she has said or done, we see her as wholly bad, and are likely to respond in a fearful, suspicious or hostile manner.

Survivors who have borderline personalities tend to split their sense of self into wholly good and wholly bad as well. For many of us, the sense of badness is so great that we feel we need to resort to extreme measures to try to keep what feel like chaotic emotions under control. Sometimes we hurt ourselves, either as a punishment or as a means of discharging negative feelings that have no other way of finding a release. Sometimes, our sense of self-hatred may be so great that we think about or attempt to take our own lives. Tragically some of us succeed.

This kind of chaotic flipping between different ways of seeing people and different emotional responses happens because of a fundamental split in how we see ourselves and how we see the world. In other words, there is a dissociation – a disconnection between one part of our personality and another.

In terms of our vase image, borderline personality is like a vase that has been cracked and actually split into two. The vase is no longer able to contain the water that is put into it, and there are times when even moving it slightly may cause it to break into two pieces. Those pieces can still be fitted back together again, but the vase as a whole is always in danger of breaking again for the very slightest of reasons.

Dissociated identities

I am seeing a young woman in her late twenties for psychotherapy. I will call her Janet. She has come because she suffers from huge anxiety, despite holding down a responsible professional role. She describes her parents as being kind and good people, but says she doesn't feel they really understand her. She says it is because she isn't a good enough daughter. Over the course of a few sessions, as we try to locate the source of her anxiety, I become aware that whenever I ask her about when she first began to feel anxious, she goes sort of blank or absent, as if she isn't really present. After a while she comes back to herself, but often doesn't seem to remember what I have been saying in the intervening few minutes. One day she goes 'blank' quite early on in the session, and as she does so, she slips off the chair and sits on the ground with her back to the wall, her head tucked down and her arms around her knees. I think to myself that she looks like a small child. I feel as if I should try to get her to come back and be present in the room.

'Janet, are you alright down there on the ground?'

She looks up, seeming slightly bewildered.

'Janet, are you alright?' I ask again.

She looks even more confused. In a little voice unlike her own she says, 'Why are you calling me Janet? My name's Felicity.'

Somehow I retain enough in the way of presence of mind to ask her how old she is. She tells me she is eight-and-a-quarter years old. I ask her what she's doing on the ground. She looks a bit confused again.

'I'm hiding in the wardrobe so they don't find me.'

Everything about her body language, her facial expression and her tone of voice says that she is a little girl rather than a grown woman. We have a few more exchanges before the blank look comes over her again, and she comes to with a start, looking like a grown-up sitting rather uncomfortably on the floor. It becomes clear that she has absolutely no memory of what has been happening for the last fifteen minutes. In fact, she doesn't really want to believe it is true.

When we were abused from a very early age, and we found ourselves in inescapable danger for a very long period of our lives, our personalities sometimes become compartmentalised in such a profound way that it is as if our personalities have fractured into a number of different parts. Each of these parts takes on an autonomous identity or sense of self. Each part is capable of operating more or less independently of the other parts. Sometimes these different parts of the self may be purely functional, in that each of them carries out a different role in our lives. At other times, they may take on an identity of their own, almost as if they were separate people living inside our body.

This type of disconnection between the different parts of our personality or identity used to go by the name multiple personality disorder, but in more recent years has become known as *dissociative identity disorder* or DID.

Survivors with DID typically experience a number of different personality states, which alternately seem to take control of their awareness or consciousness. Sometimes these different parts present as being of different ages. They may call themselves by different names. They may be aware of different personal histories. Some may have skills or knowledge that the others lack. Sometimes the different parts may call themselves by different names. Some of these different dissociated parts have no knowledge of any other part. Sometimes they may have knowledge of other parts but not have any control over what they say or do.

This may seem very far-fetched and alien to those supporting survivors, but the thing to remember is that this is just an extreme form of the type of disconnection and dissociation experienced by all survivors of childhood abuse. In fact, it is an extreme form of the sort of dissociation that is experienced from time to time by everyone, whether they were abused or not. Remember motorway amnesia? While part of our personality was absent, another part was able to drive quite safely. This is not a million miles away from the story of Janet, who held down a responsible job even if she was plagued with anxiety, but who under some circumstances went away while a little eight-year-old girl called Felicity took over her awareness.

Most people with DID do not have just one other dissociated part. There may be anything from three or four up to several dozen, or even, on rare occasions, hundreds. Some of these present as children or teenagers, while others are adults. Usually, those with DID have experienced being abused in horrific ways, almost always within their immediate family. Some, with dozens or hundreds of parts, may have been abused by an organised group. Occasionally those groups are like cults or some sort of occult group.

This level of dissociation is always a sign that the survivor has experienced some of the most extreme forms of abuse. It isn't common, but also it isn't as rare as we might think. Most survivors with DID have no idea that their personality is split into multiple parts. Their dissociative coping mechanisms work quite well, and it is only when something happens to destabilise the situation that things begin to change. Often when survivors no longer feel they have to protect these dreadful secrets for their own safety do the different parts of the personality feel safe enough and able enough to make themselves known and to get some help.

The thing that we really need to understand is that for those of us with DID, the various disconnected parts of our soul show a large degree of autonomy in how they think, feel and perceive things, what they remember, what skills they have and how they behave. In other words, they appear to have their own identity.

To give you an idea just how complete the sense of autonomy and identity can be in these circumstances: I once worked with a survivor who had a number of fully dissociated child parts, all frozen at various ages. Among these was a seventeen-year-old who had very suicidal tendencies, a thirteen-year-old who was very sensible and practical, and a fairly happy and chirpy five-year-old. Late one evening I received a distressed call from this person, but it wasn't the adult I had on the phone, it was the five-year-old. She said, 'I'm in a place with bright lights and people wearing different coloured clothes.' I asked her if she was in the hospital, and if the people in different coloured clothes were nurses and doctors. She said, 'Maybe, I don't know, but they asked me how old I was and I told them, and now everyone is cross with me.' Eventually, the sensible thirteen-year-old came to the surface and explained what had happened. The seventeen-year-old part had taken an overdose, but once she had taken it, that part disappeared back inside and the thirteen-year-old took over. Being practical and sensible, the thirteen-year-old decided to go to the hospital. This was all well and good, but while she was waiting to be seen, the five-year-old spotted some children's toys and, because she wanted to play with them, came to the surface, forcing the thirteen-year-old back inside. So when the staff came to ask her date of birth, all she was able to tell them was, 'I'm five,' which understandably sounded ridiculous to the staff, who quickly became impatient with her. We agreed on the phone that the thirteen-year-old was going to stay in charge for now, and do all the things that needed to be done to deal adequately with the hospital bureaucracy.

One point that does need to be made is that some churches and leaders tend to view these other parts of the personality as demonic spiritual forces. I have over the years had to argue with a number of church leaders and prayer ministers that what they are seeing is not a demon, but is actually a small, frightened child frozen in time at the point where horrific trauma occurred. As such they need to be dealt with in a loving and nurturing way. Attempting to do deliverance ministry may drive that part underground, but it will not get rid of it, and it will most likely do considerable damage to someone who has already experienced an appalling level of trauma.

The experience of DID is a little like our vase that has been repeatedly hit until it has not just cracked but has shattered into pieces. Those pieces are scattered around, and looking at them it is hard to see how they could be fitted back together again. However, with time, perseverance and skilled help, a full repair is possible.

Structural disconnection

When we are looking at the ways in which our soul can be fractured, it is helpful if we can think of it in terms of how the different structures of our mind, personality and even our identity can be disconnected. As I keep saying, there is nothing haphazard about these different types of disconnection. Every crack or split in the personality is there for a reason, and every one of them serves a purpose.

Of course, the degree of disconnection is always going to be more obvious in those of us who are dissociating to a high degree, but these same structural disconnections can be seen in all of us who have experienced abuse or indeed any form of trauma in childhood.

There are two ways in particular that survivors experience this sort of structural disconnection: as if they have a child frozen inside, and as if they have parts embodying specific functions.

The inner child

When we were abused as children it is likely that a part of our soul became dissociated at that point and was frozen in time. Something of our experience as an abused child – memories, emotions, perceptions and so on – stayed the same. While the rest of us grew up, that part stayed hidden inside our unconscious mind and wasn't able to grow or move on. Sometimes this is known as having an *inner child*. As well as reacting to what has happened, our inner child filters present-day events, relationships and interactions through their own experience. Something happens in the present day, and the hurt child inside us tries to fit it into their traumatised world view. That part of us responds to the present-day situation with reactions that are in fact more appropriate to the past.

Our inner child can make its presence known in a number of ways. Sometimes it can appear as a figure in dreams. At other times it can show itself in eruptions of emotions that are inflated with regard to the situations that have triggered them – in other words, we find ourselves experiencing childlike levels of anger, fear and sadness. Sometimes we can be caught up in repeating cycles of self-defeating experiences and behaviours, just as if the child frozen inside us is acting out their pain, distress and neediness.

For example, if as a child a survivor was hurt by a man with a shaved head and a loud voice, it is possible that whenever the adult survivor encounters someone with those same features or characteristics the child will react. We have talked about triggers before, but what we need to understand is that it is usually not the adult parts of our personality that are triggered, rather it is our frozen inner child who is triggered and responds in the way they would have done, or perhaps needed to at that age.

Just to be clear, many people have an inner child, even if they have not been abused as children. Any accidental or incidental trauma someone experienced as a child, particularly if the emotions were not able to be expressed and to receive an appropriate response from caregivers, may well result in a slightly split-off inner child being created. It is also important for us to understand that a person with an inner child may respond unconsciously like a child, but they do not necessarily feel themselves to be a child – they do not take on the identity of a child.

I worked with one person whose mother died quite suddenly when she was young, and for various reasons she had not been allowed to grieve, and her feelings about this very traumatic loss were not recognised or valued. She presented for therapy with anxiety, a great deal of which was focused around her own children and her relationship with them. She was always concerned that something was wrong with the children. She worried about their behaviour or whether they were suffering the early stages of some mental health problem. From time to time she would find herself losing her temper with them over what was in fact very normal behaviour for children of that age, and would even throw tantrums that were very reminiscent of a small child looking for attention. Both the concern and the tantrums were something she would never have felt able to express as a child. Those things were not really emotions and behaviours belonging to the adult. Rather it was the child showing the concern she was feeling about herself and the emotions she had never been allowed to express.

When we were abused, however, and in particular when we experienced any of the complicating factors around the abuse, our inner child is likely to exist as a much more complex and concrete part of our personality. If we were abused over a long period of time, in many ways, or by different people, we may well have a number of inner children. Each of these inner children may have been split off and frozen in time at the ages they were when they were abused in new ways or by different people.

The functional model

The different disconnected parts of our personality also each fulfil different functions. All the parts of our personality were originally split off in order to fulfil one primary mission – to keep us as safe and stable as possible under the dangerous circumstances in which we found ourselves. Every part of us has a role and a function in keeping the whole system stable. Those roles may change or even become redundant as we grow up. Over time, what were adaptive and helpful roles may become maladaptive and less helpful. Nevertheless, each part of us is still trying to fulfil its role and function.

These same parts of us, with these same general roles and functions, exist in all of us who have been abused as children. If we have dissociated identities it may be clearer and more obvious. But even if we do not, the same parts exist though in a slightly less defined way.

Public parts
These are the parts of our personality that we most often need when dealing with the outside world. We may have just one public part or we may switch between a number of them depending on what situation we find ourselves in. We may, for example, have a part of us that goes to work and deals with everything we need to do there, and another that navigates social situations.

Trauma-carrying parts

As the name suggests, these parts are those that carry the experience of the trauma that we experienced. Despite the fact that we may have little or no memory of some of our traumatic experiences, nothing is ever lost. Everything is carried somewhere in our unconscious minds – all the memories, the physical sensations, and all of the emotions connected to the traumatic events. However, these traumatic experiences tend to be split between a number of different parts. Different inner child parts will carry the memories of the trauma from different ages. Sometimes, there is a part to carry the emotions of each experience and another to carry the physical sensations. Sometimes there may be a part for each emotion. Survivors are all unique, so different people may structure things in different ways, but what is common to all is that our minds have unconsciously arranged things in such a way that no part is completely overwhelmed by the memories of the trauma they are carrying.

At times I have worked with survivors who have a whole range of trauma-carrying parts – one who carries the fear associated with a traumatic event, another who carries the sadness associated with that event, another who carries the physical sensations, and still another who may give quite a dispassionate account of the facts about what happened.

Specialist function parts

Over time, because we learned how to dissociate so early on in our lives, we may begin to split off parts of our personality to meet any new challenge. For those of us at the nearer end of the dissociative spectrum, the degree of splitting is less, so that although we still have these parts, they are far less autonomous, and so we have to learn to adapt to new situations and challenges. For those of us at the far end of the dissociative spectrum, we may lack the capacity to adapt, and instead split off new parts to deal with new situations.

Over time some of those specialist function parts are no longer needed, but they remain inside as disconnected parts of our soul. I once worked with a survivor who was a scientist. She was very good at what she did, but was finding it difficult to get jobs. This was because she had split off a part when she began to learn the science, but that part had absolutely nothing in the way of social skills. She also had a part that had learned to function in social situations. As a result, whenever she had to go for a job interview, if the part that had the social skills was on top, she couldn't answer any of the technical scientific questions. On the other hand, if the part that could handle the technical scientific questions was on top, she was hopeless at making herself engaging and likeable. The dilemma was eventually solved by facilitating the cooperation of the two parts with one another.

Guardian parts
Guardian parts effectively sit between the public parts and all the other parts inside. They have one primary function, which is to guard against our public parts becoming aware of our other parts inside, and in particular our trauma-carrying parts. This is because they believe, with some justification, that our stability depends on the parts that have to function in the outside world remaining ignorant

of all the trauma, or if they have to be aware, at least not engaging with its associated pain and distress.

Different guardian parts may have been created when we were different ages. But even when we grew up, those guardian parts remained active inside us. They can manifest in a number of different ways. Some of the more common are that they numb or suppress emotions that are rising up from the trauma-carrying parts inside. At other times they may present as quite hostile or angry, in particular when they perceive people as getting too close to the survivor, either physically or emotionally. Guardians often have a great deal invested in maintaining emotional distance. If they let people – whether friends, partners, supporters or therapists – in too close, there is a danger that some of the trauma-carrying parts inside may try to make a connection with the other person, raising the spectre of the secrets of the trauma they have experienced leaking out to the public parts.

Our essential wholeness

All of these cracked and broken parts of ourselves have meaning and purpose in our lives. They broke in response to the abuse we experienced, and they have broken in ways that reflect some of the underlying structures of our brains. This is good news, because it means that no matter how broken we may feel to ourselves or seem to others, there is an underlying wholeness to the ways in which we have fractured in response to the abuse. In other words, there is an essential wholeness to our being. It may seem to be broken beyond repair, but even our brokenness reflects the incredible way in which we were designed.

Most of the fractured parts of us are actually attempting to preserve the safety and security of our whole being. When we are under threat, and particularly when we were abused, the different parts of our brains respond in different ways; we have already seen how the different parts of the brain either go into overdrive or go into shutdown when we are faced with a threat or when we are triggered. It is important for us, and for those supporting us, to understand that the various dissociated parts of our personality are built upon these different responses that our brain has to threat and danger.

Recent theories about trauma and dissociation suggest that there are five types of responses our brain makes when we are in danger, and all of the dissociated parts of our personalities are based on these five types of response.[14]

Fight

One response in the face of threat is to fight back in whatever ways we know how. When we were abused we were too little to do that effectively, but the impulse was there nevertheless. When our souls are fractured there will be parts that are hostile, angry or even aggressive. Those parts try to protect our whole being by pushing away and resisting anything that might look or feel like a threat. That could easily include those people who are trying to help or support us. Sometimes these *fight parts* will believe that the best way to protect themselves is to pretend nothing happened to us, and anyone wanting to help threatens that coping strategy.

---

[14] Janina Fisher, *Healing the Fragmented Selves of Trauma Survivors* (London: Routledge, 2017).

Flight

Another response in the face of threat is to run away and hide. Again, when we were abused we may not have been able to find any safe place where we could hide and feel safe, but the drive to do so is incredibly strong. When something happens to trigger us, even as adults, we may disconnect and hide. We withdraw and wrap ourselves in a duvet, and hope the world and the threat that it contains will go away. We may also disconnect and hide from those who are trying to help us. This isn't because we are being difficult; it is because having to face the things that have happened to us can feel as if it threatens to destabilise us.

Freeze

Sometimes we just freeze when faced with a threat. We are like a rabbit in the headlights, unable to move, sometimes even unable to speak. It is as if a part of us believes that if we stay very still the threat will ignore us and go away. Sadly, for most of us as children that was not actually true. However, the freeze response can still pay off because when we are frozen we are unable to resist, and for some of us, not resisting the abuse was important, because it meant that we did not get even more badly hurt.

Submit

Another response is to submit and cooperate with what happens to us. When we were abused as children, particularly if we were sexually abused, we learned that submitting and cooperating pleased our abusers and may have meant that we were not hurt in worse ways. Even now in the face of threat or fear of another person, we will try to please them or placate them in some way. This can become a general strategy for how we deal with challenging situations and people in our lives. I have had therapy clients whose *submit parts* would try to please me or keep me happy – perhaps by buying me gifts, especially if they felt like they had got something wrong or made a mistake.

Attach

One person I worked with as a therapist, when she was triggered, would literally cling on to my trouser leg, just as a little girl might do when she feels scared. When I spoke to that part of her, she told me she was three years old, even though my client was actually in her late forties.

As children we are wired to need love, nurture, affection and affirmation. Even if we did not receive it, we still needed it and something deep inside us knew that we were missing out. Perhaps we were driven to form an attachment to a parent, sibling or other grown-up, who wasn't abusive to us, or who at least was less obviously abusive than others. Sometimes now we are adults we may find ourselves feeling and acting as if we were that small child desperate for love and care. We may attach ourselves to whoever seems to be the strongest or safest person in our lives. Sometimes our *attach parts* will physically cling to someone they see as safe, in a way that is more appropriate to a scared child.

Survivor Resources: Processing triggers and flashbacks

When something reminds me of a traumatic, painful or scary experience, I may be flooded with memories, sensations, thoughts and feelings that are similar to the ones I experienced at the time. This can happen when I am awake as if it is still happening, or when I am asleep – like a nightmare. These are called flashbacks, and they can feel incredibly overwhelming.

My instinct is to avoid the triggers and memories whenever possible. It's a natural response. I want to avoid pain and distress as much as I can. However, avoiding doesn't stop me being triggered again, and it doesn't stop me having flashbacks. In fact, though it may sound strange, avoiding the triggers makes it more likely that I will have flashbacks, not less.

The solution is a bit counterintuitive. Instead of avoiding, I need to lean into. It sounds a bit crazy, and it certainly isn't easy, but it does work. Gradually, with the support of my therapist and safe friends, I can learn to engage with the triggers and to process them. Here are some ways I can do this safely.

Use my grounding techniques

The grounding techniques I have learned are not a complete solution. They are kind of like first aid. They will stop things getting worse. Grounding techniques help to calm things down, and they help me to keep going long enough so that other things have a chance to work. Once I am calmer, I can begin to process and try to make sense of what is happening.

Re-frame it

As soon as I can think a bit more clearly again, there are a number of things I can remind myself about that will help me to get a different perspective.

Most importantly, I can remind myself that although the flashback feels very real, and may even feel as if the trauma is still happening, the reality is that it is just a memory – even though it may be a very unpleasant one.

I can remind myself that it doesn't belong in the here and now. The things that I am remembering actually happened somewhere else, perhaps even a long way away. They also happened a long time ago, and even though the memories can feel very present, they are actually of something that belongs in the past.

I can remind myself that the flashback doesn't mean I am going mad, even though it may be very frightening and leave me feeling a bit crazy. Rather, it represents a memory or an experience that my brain is now ready to process and try to make sense of. In exactly the same way that dreams are a way of processing and making sense of things we don't necessarily understand about ourselves and our daily lives, flashbacks and nightmares are a signal that my mind is ready to begin work to detoxify these memories.

Get it out of my head

Flashbacks happen because the memories of the trauma are in my head, and my mind has not yet found an effective way to process and make sense of them. That's not my fault. For most of my life I haven't been able or ready to face those things, because they are too painful and distressing. But even now I'm a bit older, the thought of facing the memories sometimes still feels too hard, so when I have a flashback everything just goes round in my head and has nowhere to go.

Somehow, I need to get the memories and the sensations out of my head, and put them where I can look at them in a safe way, without being completely overwhelmed. Ideally, I need to express the memories, experiences and feelings that have been triggered, preferably to a safe person. This helps stop it just going round in my head, and it tells my mind that someone else is helping me to carry the weight of it.

There are a number of ways I could do this. For example, I could:

- **Talk about it** with my therapist either in person or on the phone – but sometimes it's hard to find the words to say it out loud, and sometimes the conditioning to keep it secret and hidden is so strong. If this happens, it doesn't mean I've failed. It's just another indicator of how severe the trauma I experienced was. There are plenty of other things I can try.

- **Write it** and seal it in an envelope or put it in another safe space, ready to give to my therapist when I see them. This is good, because not only does it get it out of my head, it also allows me to put it safely away somewhere *outside* me. There is something powerful about symbolically sealing it up or locking it in a box. It tells my mind that the things I have written about can no longer get loose and hurt me.

- **Email or message** what I am remembering, experiencing and feeling to my therapist. I could then delete the 'sent' copy so it isn't in my space. This is another very effective way of getting things out of my head. Sometimes this can be helpful if I type on a keyboard faster than I can write longhand. It means I am less likely to censor myself, and less likely to engage too deeply with what I am writing, so I feel less distressed with it. Deleting my sent copy tells my mind symbolically that it is safe to trust the person to whom I sent it to carry it for me, until we can speak about it.

- **Draw** what I am experiencing, remembering and feeling – it doesn't have to be artistic. Stick figures and scribbles will do. Sometimes words are not enough. This is particularly true if what happened to me started when I was very little, before I talked very much. At other times the words themselves that describe what happened seem too dangerous or toxic for me to speak or write. Drawing or painting, or even using plasticine or modelling dough to represent what I remember or feel, can help me to discharge some of the pain and distress. It also helps that I can do it instinctively – using colours and shapes to express things that my conscious mind doesn't know how to engage with.

Keep it simple

Sometimes I worry that I won't be able to express what I need to say well enough. This is partly because flashbacks are chaotic and it is hard to say or express things in a way that makes sense. It may also be partly because I have been told by abusers that I am stupid, or that no one will believe what I say. Those things aren't true. Mostly I struggle because these things are hard and painful to express. I try to remember that what I say or write doesn't have to be eloquent or complete. A few words, images or feelings are a start. I can always go back later to fill in more details if I need to.

The important thing is that these are my words, my memories, my feelings and I need to express them in a way that makes sense to me. Simple usually works well, because there is less chance of things becoming distorted or confused. Perhaps my abusers used confusion to make me doubt myself, so it's important I do whatever I can to keep things clear and simple as I am getting them out of my head.

If it helps, I could try to use a very simple framework to help me structure my thoughts, memories and feelings. Something like this:

- This is what happened (the triggering event).
- This is what I saw.
- This is what I heard.
- This is what I smelled.
- This is what I felt.
- It made me remember or think about this traumatic memory or memories that happened.
- When I remembered, it made me feel or act in this particular way.

With the support of my therapist and other safe people, I can go back and fill in more details at a later time if I need to.

Be kind to myself

Sometimes even using this simple framework feels too difficult, and I'm tempted to give myself a hard time about it. After all, I'm used to being given a hard time. My abusers were not kind to me – or if they were it was mostly to manipulate me. If I made mistakes or wasn't able to do something, they may have punished me, sometimes severely. Even some of those who were supposed to have been helping me were not kind – they didn't understand or they got impatient. They may even have rejected me. This makes it even more important that I have some people around me who will be kind and care for me unconditionally. In time I will learn from them how to be kind to myself.

I try to remember that processing flashbacks is not easy. The time between the trigger and the response is very short, and the rush of memories, sensations and emotions can feel overwhelming. I will survive the flashback, just as I survived the original events that gave rise to it. But at the time it can feel almost as real as it did originally. It will take me a while to learn how to ground myself enough so that I can process this stuff. It really isn't surprising that I may from time to time fall back into my old coping mechanisms. If or when this happens it doesn't mean I've failed; it is just another part of my journey of recovery.

Supporter's Pause for Thought: Feeling overwhelmed

Jesus brings light into the darkest of places, and embraces the broken, calling them to wholeness and life. In His death, broken on a cross, He shares our pain and distress.

In His resurrection and ascension to glory, still bearing the marks of brokenness, He invites us to share in His wholeness.

- What does it mean to embrace the ministry of Jesus to those who are broken by abuse?
- What does it mean to partner with Him in bringing light to those who are held captive in darkness?
- What does it mean to reach out with Him in love to bind up the broken-hearted?

Working with those who are fractured by complex trauma is one of the most challenging and rewarding things anyone can do. However, it places incredible demands on time, commitment, emotional energy, patience and tolerance.

In order to be a channel for the healing presence and power of Jesus, you need to become more vulnerable and exposed than you could possibly have imagined.

You will become the object of intense feelings – both positive and negative. The one who is fractured may place upon you and try to act out all of their unfulfilled needs for love, security and affirmation. At the same time, they may also place upon you and act out all the fear, mistrust, possessiveness and rage that they have never been able to express openly before. Within days or even hours you may go from being (in their estimation) their closest friend and the only one who can help them, to being (in their estimation) a dangerous, manipulative person who is ruining their lives.

Sometimes you may receive phone calls, texts, emails, etc asking for help, often during antisocial hours, at weekends or even when you are on holiday. Sometimes you may receive calls, texts, emails, etc that are full of verbal abuse, blaming you for the way they are feeling, and even accusing you of damaging them. You will most likely experience your own strong feelings towards the one who is fractured. At times the drive to protect them, rescue them, fix them and love them feels almost uncontainable. At other times the feelings of frustration, anger, hurt and resentment rise up inside and threaten to spill out in all sorts of inappropriate ways. The spiritual forces that can sometimes be at work in those who are fractured frequently disrupt not just their lives but may attempt to disrupt the lives of you and your families. When those you are working with make progress, you may feel elated and excited at what God is doing. At other times you find yourself wondering why you ever got involved, and may even wish to abandon the journey and withdraw.

Working with those who are fractured is one of the most rewarding things anyone can ever do – but you need to know that it costs, because to begin and then abandon the journey part way would cause immense damage to the survivors you are trying to help.

The good news is that you do not have to do it on your own. The same Jesus who comes to bind up the broken-hearted is the Jesus who guides you and equips you to serve. He is the same Jesus who sustains you as He sustains all His sent-out ones. Remember, in doing this work you are as much on the frontlines as any of the apostles were in the early Church. As you embrace this call you will be able to say along with the apostle Paul:

> But he said to me, 'My grace is sufficient for you, for my power is made perfect in weakness.' Therefore I will boast all the more gladly about my weaknesses, so that Christ's power may rest on me.
> *2 Corinthians 12:9*

Chapter Six
Helpful Communication

Communicating clearly

I am having a conversation with a client via text message. She is feeling very low and worthless about herself, and admits that she has been self-harming that day. I try to reassure her. I tell her that that I'm not cross with her that she has self-harmed, but I don't want her to do it any more. I tell her that I want to help her to find a better way to deal with her feelings. She goes very quiet and after a while brings the conversation to a close. I'm left with the feeling that I may have missed something important, but I can't work out what it is.

Later, when I feel prompted to check to see that she is alright, she admits that she has self-harmed in quite a bad way. She tells me she thought I was telling her she had to self-harm even more than before. I am horrified, and can't understand how she could have thought such a thing.

'You told me I had to do it better,' she says.

As we pick our way through our earlier conversation, it becomes apparent that she was made to self-harm by her abusers, who would sometimes tell her that she had to do it 'better' if she hadn't hurt herself badly enough for their liking. She had interpreted my saying I wanted her to find better ways to deal with her feelings as me telling her to self-harm in a 'better' way.

Survivors of childhood abuse can often find it hard to communicate in a clear and unambiguous way. Very often we end up feeling not heard or misunderstood. Sometimes we may find ourselves offending or upsetting people without ever having intended to. We can also find ourselves feeling very confused about what is being said to us. Because of this, mix-ups and misunderstandings can be quite common, and can be a source of distress for us.

These difficulties with communication are very understandable, when we think about it in the context of what has happened to us, and how those who hurt and abused us sometimes used words. All too often, those who abused us made words dangerous. Partly this may have been because they used words to put us down or call us horrible names, but it may also have been because they used their words as another tool to manipulate and confuse us. If we were abused by people who were supposed to love us, care for us or look after us, whether it was within our immediate family or not, we were effectively trapped in those relationships, sometimes for many years, even decades. We were trapped in relationships that had pain, distress, humiliation and deception at their core. Such abuse does huge damage to our trust in people, and that damaged trust extends to the things people say. Even to this day, we may not always be sure whether it is safe to trust the things that people say to us.

However, in order to recover and heal from the abuse we experienced, we need to build healthy, supportive relationships with safe people. An essential part of this is to find ways of communicating that are clear and helpful, because healthy communication is at the heart of all supportive relationships. Unfortunately, our abusers communicated in ways that were unhelpful and unhealthy. We learned that it wasn't wise for us to trust that anything they said was true or safe. They used words in ways that were designed to confuse, deceive, trick or catch us out. When we didn't understand, or if we fell into one of the traps their words had set for us, it could cause huge confusion and distress. It became hard for us to know what was true and what wasn't. Sometimes they even punished and abused us because we didn't understand or respond in the ways they wanted us to.

Even now, we can find it hard to know how to communicate clearly, or to understand what others are saying to us. Often we can find it difficult to trust that they are saying what they really mean. We live with the constant anxiety that we are misunderstanding or getting something wrong. With that anxiety comes the expectation that we will be punished for our mistake.

Ideas for clearer communication

What we need is some ideas to help us communicate in a way that is clear and unambiguous. It is also worth remembering that the fact that we are probably not yet doing all of these does *not* mean we are getting it wrong or being bad. It is really difficult to learn a new way of communicating, and it takes time. It's not that different from learning a whole new language, but with the added complication that although a lot of the words may look the same, now they may mean very different things. Therefore, we need to be patient and give ourselves time while we are learning.

Some of these ideas may also contain words and phrases that are potentially triggering to us. In a sense this is part of the point. If we keep avoiding them, we never become desensitised to their impact, and they go on triggering us. But if we know they are coming, we can prepare and ground ourselves, and take more steps in learning to communicate in helpful and healthy ways.

Take things at face value

Even though our abusers communicated in ways that were deceptive and manipulative, most other people do not. This is particularly true of those who are helping us – our therapists, supporters and friends. Even though it is hard to trust, we do our best to try to believe that what they say is what they mean. We do our best to trust their good heart and good faith towards us, and to believe that there are no hidden meanings in what they say. We do our best to believe that they are not trying to trick us, or manipulate us into doing something that will get us into trouble.

If our therapists or supporters ask how we are doing, we can assume they really want to know. We can also assume that they want to know because they genuinely care for us. This means we don't have to hide or minimise what we are feeling or whatever may be going on for us. It is safe for us to speak and to tell them all of what we are thinking or feeling.

If our therapists or supporters express care for us or affirmation towards us, it isn't because they are lying, or

163

for any underhand reason. It may not make sense to us, and it may not be easy for us to believe, especially to begin with, but the truth is they are most likely sincere in what they say. Even if we find it hard to accept or believe, perhaps we can suspend judgement for a while, and give ourselves time to see if their actions and attitudes go along with their words.

The truth is not everyone will always communicate clearly with us. Sometimes people will ask how we are doing, and if we tell them they may get that look on their face that lets us know they weren't really expecting us to share what we have. This is not because they are bad or trying to deceive or trick us. It is simply because most people don't understand just how important clear communication is to us. When we choose the people who are going to be our supporters, it is so important that they understand about the best ways to communicate with us. Perhaps we can get them to read this chapter or at least the parts that feel relevant, so they will know what it is we need from them.

Use appropriate channels of communication

Different channels of communication have their strengths and weaknesses. Some may make us feel safer, while others may make it easier to say complicated things in a clear manner. Therefore, wherever possible it is important for us to try to use the most appropriate channels of communication for the things we want to talk about.

Face-to-face

The advantage of in-person communication is that it is much easier for us to pick up the non-verbal cues that are an important part of conveying meaning clearly. It is estimated that up to 80 per cent of the meaning in any conversation doesn't actually come from the words that are said, but by non-verbal means such as body language, tone of voice and facial expression. If we are face to face with people it is much easier for both us and them to understand what is being said, and there is much less chance of getting mixed up and confused.

However, there are some disadvantages to in-person communication as well. One disadvantage is simply that it isn't always convenient or appropriate for quick conversations. We can use face-to-face communication for conversations where we need plenty of time in order to feel safe and held. In terms of talking with our therapists and supporters this is especially true when we need to talk about difficult stuff or express strong feelings. In other words, if we are wanting to have a conversation where there is potentially a lot of emotional content, or if we need to feel that someone is very present for us, face-to-face is always going to be the best option.

There is a slight irony that the very things that can make face-to-face communication helpful for having difficult or emotionally charged conversations can also at times make it more difficult to have those conversations. Sometimes, the very nature of the things we need to share can cause us to feel shame or embarrassment. Although in an ideal world talking about these things in person might be the best, it may be too big a leap for us if we are disclosing things that make us feel very vulnerable. On these occasions it may feel easier to use one of the less personal means of communication first, so we can test the water, before following up with a conversation in person.

Calls

There are a number of advantages to talking on the phone. One of the most obvious is that it gives us a means of connecting, even when we are not physically close to the person on the other end. So much of our journey of healing and recovery depends on us being able to make meaningful and healthy connections with others. There may be times when we desperately need some human contact with someone we trust, but for whatever reason actually seeing them in person is impossible or less convenient. At least on the phone we can hear their voice and we can pick up from their tone that we are still connected. We can also pick up something of the emotional currents underneath the surface of the conversation. It can also be reassuring when we are struggling or feeling a bit out of control to hear the voice of someone we trust, and who we know cares about us.

The disadvantage of talking on the phone is that we can easily miss some of the more visual non-verbal cues. Also, the phone isn't always convenient or private. The phone is never going to be a substitute for in-person communication; however, it can be something of a lifeline for us, a way for us to stay connected and feel supported when we might otherwise feel isolated and cut off.

Email

The benefits of email in terms of instant communication are fairly obvious, but it can be particularly helpful for us on our journey of recovery and healing. This is partly because it allows us to do two things that are harder to do via other means of communication. The first is to communicate in a slightly longer form. When I was a therapist back in the 1990s, email was more or less unheard of. I often used to encourage my more traumatised clients to write down their thoughts and feelings and send them to me in between sessions, but it could easily take two or three days for their letters to reach me. During that time they would often be wracked with anxiety about what they had said and how I might respond to it.

With email we know that once it has been sent, it will be received pretty much immediately. However, we can take our time over what we want to say. Sometimes that helps us feel less under pressure than we might when trying to come up with the right words straight away. We can take time to think and reflect, and find the words and phrases that feel most right to us. It also helps that we can convey meaning not only through what we say, but how we say it, and the style of writing we use.

Email is also a form of communication that is uninterrupted. For some of us, the abuse we suffered meant that we were silenced or not listened to. It may have meant that when we tried to speak we were shut down or talked over. Being able to say what we need to and know that no one can shut us down can be really healing.

Email can also be really helpful if we need to share something that feels too hard to share face to face at first, particularly if it is something that needs to be explained in any detail. For some of us, saying the wrong thing meant being punished or hurt in other ways when we were children. Email allows us just enough distance to share the scary stuff without fear of being hurt.

The disadvantage of email is that it is inevitably slightly less personal. This means that most of the non-verbal cues are lost, so although we may be able to communicate something in the way of emotional tone through our style of writing, few of us are gifted enough as writers to be able to do so perfectly. Therefore, it may often feel harder to convey and to understand emotional depth and subtlety than if we use more immediate forms of communication.

Text

The advantage of text or other messaging apps is that they are great for quick communication, especially when we are in the middle of doing other things. We can send and receive messages without others necessarily being aware. This makes text messaging great for quick requests for reassurance, or to let people know how we are feeling, or what we are struggling with as we go through our day. It is also helpful as it allows those supporting us to give quick replies and reassurance even if they are busy.

The group chat options on some messaging apps are also useful as it means we can let all those who are supporting us know what is happening very quickly, and receive responses, reassurance or advice from a number of different sources.

The disadvantage is that all of the subtle nuances of meaning are lost. Also, using small keyboards, mistypes are very common, which can drastically alter meaning.

Therefore, it is very easy to be misunderstood or to misunderstand. This doesn't mean text is wrong; it is just that we need to know its limitations. It is best used for exchanging short information, general conversation, or just to help us feel more connected and less alone.

Avoid euphemisms

Sometimes we can fall into the habit of using 'shorthand' words and phrases or euphemisms to talk about the trauma and abuse that we have experienced. There can be a few different reasons why we do this, and it isn't necessarily wrong in itself. However, it is important for us to think about why we feel the need to do this, and whether using such euphemisms is actually helpful to us or not. It's also worth us thinking about the fact that sometimes the use of shorthand can make misunderstandings and miscommunication more likely.

Sometimes we use shorthand forms to refer to things simply for convenience. Perhaps there are things about the trauma we experienced that we have talked about, and possibly worked through to some extent. It can be helpful for us to have a way of referring to these things without having to get too specific, and knowing that the person we are talking with will understand what we are saying.

For example, I worked with a survivor who was abused in many ways throughout her childhood right up until she left home. Even as an adult, the abusers sometimes found her and hurt her. She often would have flashbacks or bad dreams about what had happened to her. While we were working through some of the abusive memories she had, she sometimes found it more convenient to refer to a flashback or dream using one of a few shorthand phrases. She would talk about a flashback as having been about 'recent' things – meaning things that happened after she left home, 'long ago' things – meaning things that happened when she was an older child and teenager, or 'long, long ago' – meaning things that happened when she was a small child. Sometimes she would also mention a particular person or a location. This was helpful, because it allowed her to give me information about things that she had shared, but which were still really hard for her to talk about. We used the shorthand not as a way of avoiding talking about the incidents, but as a slightly gentler way into talking about them.

However, there may be times when using shorthand forms to talk about things, particularly traumatic events or our reactions to them, can be a way of not saying or not engaging with things in the way we need to. Shorthand and euphemisms can mean that we don't allow ourselves to be in touch with our emotions, and of course there can be times when that is necessary. It's not necessarily a bad thing to want to avoid being triggered or to manage our emotional responses, especially when we need to be functional in the world at large. But there are times when our healing and recovery process means that we need to feel those things, and allow ourselves to talk about them in more depth. At those times, the use of shorthand or euphemisms is perhaps less helpful, and may be better avoided.

Another reason to avoid the use of shorthand forms and euphemisms, especially when talking about our experiences of abuse, is that we can end up mirroring something our abusers did to us. Our abusers almost certainly used words to cover up and distort what they were doing to us. Their intention in using those words and phrases was to try to make it sound to us and to themselves as if what they were doing – the abuse they were perpetrating on us – was in some way normal or OK. Of course, different abusers use different words and phrases, but their intent was always the same – to minimise or normalise the abuse.

There are so many deceptive phrases that those who abused us may have used to wriggle out of being honest about what they were doing to us. It is impossible to list all the variations that I have heard both as a survivor and as a therapist working with survivors. However, these few may give a flavour of the sort of thing we're talking about:

- 'Being a good girl/boy' = doing what our abusers wanted/not resisting
- 'Our little secret' = sexual abuse
- 'Discipline/punishment' = serious physical assault

The thing is that we tend to do the same. Because of the shame we feel, and the secrecy we were forced to keep, we ourselves come up with all sorts of shorthand and euphemisms to describe what happened to us, and some of the impact it has on us. Again, there are way too many variations on these to list here, but these few will give an idea:

- 'The thing that happened…' = a particular example of abuse

- 'Messing up/being stupid/making a mistake' = self-harming or putting ourselves at risk
- 'Bad stuff/yucky things' = memories of being abused or hurt

If we can use the proper words and phrases to describe things, it will help us in a number of ways. For example: 'I dreamed about some bad things, and when I woke up I messed up,' becomes, 'I dreamed about being sexually abused, and was so upset when I woke up that I self-harmed'.

It makes what we are trying to talk about clear to those who are trying to help us. The clearer we can be, the more they understand us, and the more they understand us, the more they can help. If we are not clear and they misunderstand, they can easily miss the fact that we are asking them to help us in some way. They can also end up trying to help us in the wrong ways or about the wrong things. Those sorts of miscommunication can lead to some real problems in our relationship with those who are helping and supporting us.

Using the proper words and phrases to describe things can also begin to desensitise us to the triggering effect of those words and phrases. When we habitually use euphemisms and shorthand terms to describe what happened to us, we can find ourselves not just being triggered by reminders of the abuse we experienced, but even by the words themselves. It is almost as if we start to have a phobic reaction to the words as well as to the memories of the events. Therefore we need to detoxify the words, so that they don't remain as a source of triggers for us.

One of the things abusers are very successful in doing is drawing us into unwitting collusion with them. As we start to use the proper words and phrases to describe what they did to us rather than using euphemisms, it stops the process whereby we automatically minimise or normalise the awful things they did to us. This in turn allows us to fully acknowledge to ourselves and to others that what happened to us was wrong. This is an essential step in our journey of recovery and healing.

When we call things by their proper names it has a huge positive impact on our sense of self-worth. So much of the trauma we experienced was surrounded by lies and distortions; so much so that it can sometimes feel as if we ourselves cannot tell truth from fiction. When we use the proper words and phrases it helps us to value ourselves. We are worth so much more than the lies and deception our abusers put on us. When we acknowledge our truth, it counteracts some of the degrading and devaluing effects of what they did.

Speaking out our truth helps us to take ownership of our actions. One of the ways our abusers distorted the truth was to convince us that we would be shamed if anyone knew what they did to us. So we learned to hide not only what they did, but also our responses to it. Often we were driven into self-defeating and even self-punishing coping strategies. The shame we felt caused us to hide those things as well. Acknowledging our truth helps us to break out of that trap, and to find healthier ways to cope and manage ourselves.

Sometimes we hide and minimise what has happened, even from the people who are there to help and support us – such as our therapists and supportive friends. This may partly be because we fear that something bad will happen to those we share with. Perhaps that sounds a bit irrational, but for many of us it is completely understandable. Those memories of what was done to us cause us pain, distress and even harm. They are so strong and powerful that often it feels as if we cannot contain them, or as if they are visible to others. It isn't surprising, therefore, for us to worry that sharing those things will have an equally damaging effect on them. The reality of course is that simply telling people about what happened to us will not hurt or damage them. However, to know that in practice rather than theory, we need to see that those who are helping and supporting us can cope with the things we tell them, and that they will not be overwhelmed or damaged.

Ask for help

When we were being hurt and abused as children, the chances are that there was no help available to stop what was happening. For many of us, even if we worked up the courage to ask for help, we weren't taken seriously. We may even have been disbelieved by those we needed to help us. This experience of help not being available when we needed it can make it hard for us to ask for help now, or even to know when it is appropriate for us to ask for help.

Sometimes we were faced with an almost impossible dilemma. We needed to ask for help, but our abusers made it clear that we had to keep what they were doing to us secret, otherwise there would be dire consequences. We tried to signal our need for help without risking our abusers knowing. We did it in all sorts of different ways – through our behaviour, through illness, through being accident prone, or through outbursts of emotion that we couldn't explain. Perhaps we tried to explain to someone, without necessarily having to say it out loud. We hoped that someone would understand and investigate further. We hoped that they would see that we needed something from them. But all too often our signals were misunderstood, and the help we were hoping for never materialised.

Sometimes even now we find it hard to ask for help directly. We still try to signal our distress and pain, perhaps without even knowing consciously that this is what we are doing. But unfortunately, people still often miss the point, and they fail to understand properly what it is we are trying to say or what we need. Sometimes, we convince ourselves that we have no needs, and this is what we portray to our friends and the world around us. It means we never need to feel the disappointment of being misunderstood or let down. But deep down we know this isn't actually true. In reality the needs of the hurt and abused child we were are still there inside us, and though we do everything we can to keep it covered over, we are desperate for someone to notice, to understand, and to meet those needs.

Somehow we have to find a way to break out of this self-defeating cycle of needing help but not knowing how to ask for what we need.

If we can learn to ask for help directly and unambiguously that is great, but for most of us that is going to take a while. Therefore, until we are able to get to that point, we can agree with our therapists and supporters some appropriate ways to signal that we need some input, communication or support. Sometimes this could be as simple as being able to text a single word or an emoji. It is also going to help both us and those who are helping and supporting us, if we can agree what type of response we will get if we ask for help – eg will it be a text, a call or a visit?

It is also important for those who are helping us to understand that just because we need something, it doesn't necessarily mean we know what sort of thing it is we need. Sometimes when they ask us what we need, we simply don't know or can't express it. We don't need to worry – they know we are not being deliberately difficult. We can agree ahead of time what suggestions or responses they could make. If what they suggest is not right for us at that moment it is OK to say so. They are not going to get cross with us, hurt us or abandon us – though we may find that hard to believe, and we may need a lot of reassurance about that.

Check it out

Because of what our abusers did to us, when we try to communicate, everything we say has to go through a lot of filters. These filters make it easy for us to jump to conclusions or to misunderstand. From time to time we may get very scared, and start worrying that those who are helping and supporting us may be saying things that agree with or confirm our abuser's view of us. We may interpret the things they say as being critical, demeaning or threatening. Some of us who may have been given an exaggerated view of our abuser's power might even worry in case those who are trying to help us are actually somehow in league with our abusers.

I have worked with many survivors who sometimes misunderstood what I was saying as supporting some of these beliefs. As a survivor myself I know that there can still be a tendency to read into the things that people say, and jump to the wrong conclusion. It is a type of hypervigilance that goes with the trauma we suffered. We are on the lookout for the signs and patterns that might give us some warning that we are about to be hurt or abused again. We may know in some part of us that these worries and fears are not rational, and don't reflect the current truth. At the same time there may be other parts of us that are so scared we find it almost impossible to think rationally or to remember that the people supporting and helping us are different from those who abused and hurt us.

When this happens, the first thing we need to do is to check it out. The chances are that we have misunderstood something, and the things we are worrying about are not actually true. For most things, when we are not sure what is being said, if we ask then we will be reassured. We can find out what is really being said, and then we will know and can stop worrying.

We can also find ourselves believing a lot of other things too that are not necessarily directly related to those helping or supporting us. This is because our abusers lied to us and in other ways distorted the truth a lot of the time. For example, they may have told us that terrible things would happen, either to us or to the people we told, if we spoke up or didn't keep things hidden. We need to try to remember that much of what our abusers said to us was not reliable. Either it was not true or at best it was a distortion of the truth. Even if it was true once, it certainly isn't true now. A lot of it isn't even logical. But because they said this stuff when we were little, we believed it, and it is easy for us to continue to believe it now.

These are the sorts of things we need to check out as well. It doesn't have to be complicated. We can just ask simple questions: *If I do this, does it mean that something bad will happen?* When we are asking these sorts of questions, it is a real case in point of trying not to use euphemisms, so that there is maximum clarity. For example, *'If I tell you what my abusers did to me, will it make you want to do it too?'*

Be nice to myself

All the time we need to keep in mind that we are changing habits and coping strategies that have been there for a long time. They served us well, or at the very least they were better than the alternatives. Many of them we have used for such a long time, we are not even consciously aware of them any more.

We need to remember that bringing change and healing to this area is not easy. We are not deliberately getting caught up in unhealthy communication styles. This has been one of the many ways we have tried to keep ourselves safe. As we work on changing our ways of communicating, we are not going to get everything right all at once. We will make mistakes and there will be misunderstandings. But mistakes and misunderstandings are not a disaster, and they don't have to cause huge problems. As long as the people who are helping and supporting us are willing to try to understand our difficulties in this area, the chances are that any miscommunication can be put right.

Sometimes people may get a bit upset if they don't understand, but the more we can explain to them and the more we can use helpful ways of communicating, the more understanding they are likely to be. Even if they don't fully understand or don't always react in the ways we would like them to, we need to try to recognise that this is a problem they have; it doesn't mean that we are wrong or bad.

Survivor Resources: Communication checklist

Here are some of the ideas for helpful communication presented as a checklist. If we feel we are getting tangled in miscommunication with those supporting us, we can work our way through this to see if there is a way to make things clearer.

1. If they are saying nice things to me or about me, I could try considering that they might actually mean it.
2. Am I using the most appropriate means of communication for what I'm trying to say?
3. Am I actually saying what I mean – using the right words, not minimising things?
4. Remember it is OK for me to ask for help.

179

5. If I don't understand what people mean, or even if I think I do but I'm worried, I can check or ask them to make it clearer.

6. Am I assuming they understand what I'm saying? Even if it seems clear and obvious to me, could I make it even clearer?

7. If there has been a misunderstanding or communication has got tangled, it's not the end of the world. We can and will sort it out.

Supporter's Pause for Thought: Watching what we say

Jesus tells us to let our yes be our yes and our no be our no (Matthew 5:37). As supporters of those who have experienced abuse, and all the lies and distortion that goes with it, how can you begin to establish clear, unambiguous and healthy communication?

Here are seven points that may help:

- Don't pretend to know what you don't know – if in doubt, ask.

- Be authentic about how things make you feel – it is OK to have an emotional reaction.

- Don't promise what you can't deliver – it may take a long time to re-establish trust.

- Don't say what you don't mean – survivors can detect insincerity a mile off.

- Don't assume they know what you mean – always check that they have understood.

- Remember that one critical word will outweigh twenty words of affirmation.

- If you make a mistake, even without intending to, apologise – this may be a new and healing experience for them.

Chapter Seven
Dealing with Shame

Abuse invades our identity

One of the most corrosive things about child abuse is the way it can invade and disfigure our identity – our sense of who we are. The things that were done to us were appalling in terms of the physical acts and the way in which our dignity was taken from us. But in a very real way the damage goes a lot deeper than that. As small babies we come into the world with a certain set of needs and expectations wired into us. The psychologist Abraham Maslow famously defined a *hierarchy of needs* that all of us need to have fulfilled if we are going to survive, grow and become all that we were created to be. We cannot develop in the areas further up the pyramid unless the following needs are adequately met.[15]

---

[15] This version of the well-known pyramid diagram is adapted from one created by an unknown person, who based it on the work of Abraham Maslow in his book *Motivation and Personality* (New York: Harper, 1954).

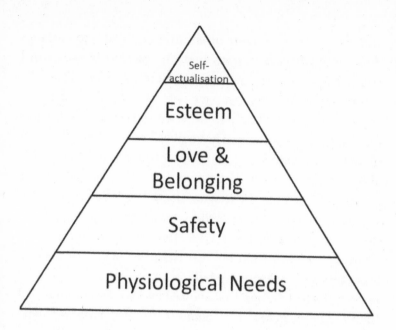

We expect that those who are taking care of us – usually our mothers and fathers – will be kind and loving. We expect that they will nurture and care for us. We expect that they will protect us and stand up for us. We expect that they will love, affirm and comfort us. Our model of the rest of the world and our relationships with others are very largely determined by whether and how those needs and expectations are met.

For some of us, the abuse and trauma we experienced did not take place within this original caring family. However, it was still a huge shock to us. It still shattered our picture of the world, and perhaps more importantly of ourselves.

For others of us the abuse we experienced happened at the hands of those who were supposed to care for us and love us. The fact that these basic expectations were not met, and were in fact overridden in the most violent and degrading of ways, means that our picture of the world and of ourselves was distorted from the very beginning.

Either way, the impact of childhood abuse is devastating, particularly to how we see ourselves. One of the things most survivors have in common is that our self-image is damaged in some very fundamental ways. We almost always choose to believe that it was we who were at fault rather than those who abused us. We believe that we are to blame for the horrible things that happened to us despite the fact that we were too young to have done anything awful enough to deserve such treatment. Sometimes the reasons we believe ourselves to be to blame are because of things that we believe we have done. *If I hadn't been naughty, I wouldn't have been punished.* The reality is that this is never true. There is nothing that we as children could have done that was so bad it justified the physical, sexual or emotional abuse that we experienced. Nevertheless, those beliefs are hard to shake. Not only did our abusers tell us we were to blame, but for a small child it almost always feels safer to blame ourselves than it does to blame an adult – particularly an adult in a role of authority or caregiving.

However, for many survivors, the belief about who was to blame for the abuse we suffered goes even deeper than the idea that we did something bad. Many of us came to believe that there was something *intrinsically* bad about us, that there was something wrong in who we were, not just in what we did. Of course, part of the reason for that is to do with what we were told. Our abusers almost certainly emotionally and verbally abused us, irrespective of which other ways they may have abused us. They almost certainly gave us the message that we were unworthy or horrible in some way, in order to try to justify the awful things they were doing to us. As well as by their actions, they used words to dehumanise us, so that they would feel less bad about how they were treating us. We came to the conclusion that we were bad. What other explanation could there be for the things they did? They did things that made us feel utterly horrible. We were afraid and filled with shame about what was happening. We didn't want to believe it could be the fault of the adults, especially if those adults were the ones who were supposed to be loving and caring for us the most. Surely it had to be something awful about us that made these things happen?

Now we are grown up, we may know rationally that these things are not true. But rational thinking has very little to do with how we feel, and especially how we feel about ourselves. Somewhere frozen inside us there is still a hurt and damaged child who believes themselves to be at fault for the things that happened and the way they feel. Whether we like it or not, there are times when it is not the rational adult part of us that has the strongest voice; rather it is the damaged child whose pain and distress sounds most loudly. Particularly for those of us for whom the abuse began very young, it can be incredibly hard to distinguish between what happened to us, how we feel and who we are. The reason for this is quite simply that when we were very young children the distinction between these things was not necessarily very clear. For all children, at the very earliest stages of our development, it takes time to separate out all of those things. But if we suffer significant levels of trauma while our mental processes are still developing, it means that part of us may become frozen at a point where there is still considerable confusion between our experience, our emotions and our identity.

In a very real sense, because the things that happened to us were horrible, and those things made us *feel* horrible, we came to believe we *are* horrible. It is quite common for survivors to conceptualise this horribleness as being an almost tangible contaminating substance or force, a bit like radioactive waste. One survivor I worked with described it simply as *yuck*. We may even come to believe that the yuck we feel on ourselves could get on to other people and in some way contaminate or damage them.

How shame attacks our life

The beliefs we hold have an impact on how we live. If one of our core beliefs is that we are infected in our innermost being with this tangible, communicable vileness, then that belief is going to have a practical effect on our lives. Many of the self-defeating and self-destructive behaviours that survivors of abuse engage in can be seen to be connected to our sense of our own worthlessness – the fact that we believe ourselves to be contaminated and damaged in our core identity.

That sense of contamination or 'yuckiness' is actually shame. Shame says that who we are is bad, worthless, unworthy of love, care and belonging. Shame says that we are dangerous to associate with, in case others are infected or contaminated by our intrinsic badness. It doesn't take a huge leap of imagination to begin to see how behaviours such as taking drugs or abusing alcohol are actually an attempt to change our mental state so that we are no longer aware of or connected with the sense of shame we feel. In effect we are attempting to self-medicate away all the shame, or failing that at least to blot out our awareness of it, the problem being with all such strategies that sooner or later we have to sober up. When we do, our awareness of the shame that we believe defines our core identity comes crashing back in. Only now, to add to the tally of how lacking in worth and useless we feel, there is the shame of having lost control and resorted to using alcohol or drugs to deal with our feelings of badness. Not to mention anything embarrassing or worse that we may have done while we were under the influence.

Sometimes we try to deal with our sense of our own badness in other, equally self-destructive and usually compulsive ways. Perhaps we self-harm in some way, through cutting or burning or hitting ourselves. This violence against ourselves seems to fulfil at least two functions. One is to let the badness out. Something about the pain, and for those of us who cut ourselves, the letting out of blood in particular, seems to help release some of the pressure of the feelings of badness and worthlessness. At the same time, hurting ourselves in any way also serves to punish us for our badness. For some of us, whenever we make a mistake or get something wrong, we feel as if we have no choice but to hurt ourselves. This is because whatever mistake it was we made, whether real or imaginary, it is evidence of our essential badness. Therefore we need to be punished, and because our abusers are mostly no longer around to hurt us again, we feel driven to punish ourselves instead.

Some eating disorders such as anorexia, bulimia and the less well known *orthorexia nervosa* can also be our desperate attempts to deal with our feelings of shame. With anorexia we are attempting both to starve the badness out of ourselves and to exert a measure of control, because our experience of abuse is that it represented such a profound loss of control over our own lives. Bulimia is similar to anorexia, except that the binge eating associated with it can be seen as an attempt to suppress our chaotic emotions, and to protect ourselves from harm. Orthorexia as a type of eating disorder has only relatively recently been identified.[16] With orthorexia people become obsessed with eating healthily, to the point where it is not healthy at all. For example, they may have an extreme diet where they attempt to cut out all foods containing fat or carbohydrate or both. In some sense the recent trend for 'clean eating' with its rejection of processed or non-natural foods has fuelled the rise in orthorexia. Not that eating healthily or 'clean' is necessarily a bad thing, but when we are using food to deal with our feelings of badness or being contaminated it can become a problem, as we restrict our food intake to such a degree that we do not get adequate nutrition, and end up with similar health issues to those of us who are anorexic.

One survivor friend of mine, who developed orthorexia to deal with her feelings of being unclean, quite literally used to have a panic attack if she was given food to eat that

---

[16] Steven Bratman with David Knight, *Health Food Junkies: Overcoming the Obsession with Healthful Eating* (New York: Broadway, 2004).

contained any fat or sugar. She saw it as being almost like the abuse she had experienced – as something that would inevitably add to her feelings of being unclean and a source of contamination.

Some of us who have survived childhood abuse may also develop conditions such as obsessive-compulsive disorder (OCD). We become convinced either that the world around us is unclean and dangerous, or that we ourselves are unclean and dangerous, or possibly both. The fear that we will contaminate other people or things, or that we ourselves will become even more contaminated, is so great that we have to develop all kinds of ritualised behaviours to make sure that we and others are safe – checking that doors are locked, that cookers are switched off, and that we have carried out activities in the right order becomes vital to help us feel secure. The problem of course is that no matter how much we check, and no matter how elaborately we carry out our rituals, none of it deals with the sense of essential badness that has come from the abuse we suffered. Therefore, we end up having to check more and more, and carry out ever more intricate and elaborate rituals in an attempt to pursue safety for ourselves and others.

Our sense of being bad or unclean can also be a component of other mental health difficulties. One survivor I worked with developed a psychotic condition in which he was convinced that people could read his mind. It was an understandable delusion. He had been sexually abused, and particularly later in his teenage years felt incredibly guilty that he hadn't resisted more, and perhaps had even cooperated to a degree. The shame and uncleanness he felt was so strong, he was convinced that others could see it on him, or read it in his mind.

Even if we don't develop recognised conditions such as eating disorders or OCD, the sense of our own essential badness and uncleanness has a negative impact on our lives. It undermines our confidence in ourselves, and makes it hard for us to connect with others, in case they discover what we fear is the awful truth about ourselves. This can affect our education, our work and our ability to form and maintain relationships.

Getting beyond the shame

Somehow as survivors we need to find ways of taking our lives back from the invasion of shame. All the strategies that we have come up with as we were growing up have helped us to manage how we feel and how we interact with the world. They have stopped us from becoming overwhelmed, and have allowed us to function to a degree. However, they have not solved the essential problem, and our sense of badness and shame remains, and continues to have a corrosive effect on our lives.

The truth is that there is no quick fix for this type of injury. We can begin, however, by recognising it as being just that: an injury inflicted on us by those who hurt and abused us. Part of our problem is that the world at large does not want to recognise the reality of childhood abuse. The world looks at it in terms of a social issue that happens somewhere else, probably to some other, most likely low-status social group. However, that is a myth.[17] The other way the rest of the world looks at the impact of abuse is in terms of illness. However, this can cause us difficulties, because illness is often seen as something that involves infection and contamination, which only serves to reinforce the belief that we are bad and probably dangerous to others. When we start to re-frame the impact of the abuse we suffered as injuries, however, we find a whole new frame of reference and more helpful ways of thinking about what has been done to us.

We have been injured by one or more violent assaults. It makes no difference whether the abuse we experienced involved actual physical actions or was emotionally or verbally violent. The fact is we suffered violence to our bodies, or our minds, and to our spirit – by which I mean our innermost being. Such violence left us wounded, physically, emotionally or spiritually, and for many of us those wounds were severe enough that they have left long-lasting scars. Just as no one can 'catch' an injury from another, no one can be infected by what was done to us. Our injuries and scars may cause others to feel sad for us, or angry on our behalf, but they cannot hurt or damage those who love us, care for and support us.

It may seem trivial to think in terms of changing the language we use to think about and speak about the badness we feel inside as a result of the abuse. But the reality is that we think in words for the most part, and the language we use has a greater impact on how we think and

[17] 'Reporting child abuse', https://www.bromley.gov.uk/info/200127/sa feguarding_children/163/reporting_child_abuse/3 (accessed 22nd May 2019).

feel than we might expect. Changing the language we use is not easy; we've been thinking in the old way for years, maybe even decades. However, gradually and with the help of loved ones, friends and supporters, we can change the way we speak and therefore, to a certain extent, the way we think about these things.

Nevertheless, we shouldn't think that this is the whole answer. There are many more factors that make us vulnerable to these feelings of badness and uncleanness. Those things had their roots in the actions and attitudes of others. There were those who abused us, and there were those who didn't recognise or who chose not to see what was happening. For us as survivors, actions and inaction speak louder than words. Whatever words were said, the actions of our abusers and the inaction, whether deliberate or simply ignorant, of those who should have stopped it, have sent their own message. It is a message that our unconscious mind has taken in and allowed to define our view of ourselves and the world. When we were victimised children we didn't have much if anything in the way of choice about who we had around us. For most of us, getting away from our abusers was simply not possible or was too dangerous. At the same time, the ignorance or deliberate not knowing of those who should have protected us was all that was available to us in terms of human connection and relationship.

Now, however, we do have a choice about who we have in our lives. It may not always be the easiest of choices to make. One of the effects of feeling that we are essentially bad is that we can come to believe that abusive relationships, or ones that are in some other way unhelpful, are all we deserve. Many of us go through periods in our lives when it seems as if every relationship and friendship we have replicates some aspect of the abuse we experienced, even if it is only that those friends and loved ones are unable or unwilling to give us the things we need to help us become whole. Again, it may not be a quick and easy process to change this pattern. However, it can be done when we begin to look at our relationships with others in a different way.

The relationships we have in our lives right now need to give us something that we didn't have when we were growing up. For many of us, when we were children we lacked people who would give us love, care, affirmation and affection with no strings attached. By definition, those who abused or neglected us gave us something that was not love. That may be hard for us to accept, because many abusers, especially those within the immediate family or close circle of friends told us that they loved us or that they were doing what they did for our own good. They may even have convinced themselves that they loved us – the human mind is capable of quite stunning levels of denial and self-deception. But love does not cause deliberate injury. Even if there were occasions when they affirmed, nurtured and cared for us, the fact that they subjected us to deliberate abuse or maltreatment undermines any idea that they truly loved us.

Love also does not ignore or turn a blind eye to the pain of a child. As well as the active abuse that we experienced, we also suffered from the enabling and silence of others. Of course, we don't want to stigmatise everyone who didn't take action to protect us as enabling or collusive.

Many people may genuinely have been ignorant of what was going on, or perhaps were too afraid for themselves to do anything about it. Nevertheless, in order to recover and heal now, we need people in our lives who will be actively engaged and interested in what is happening to us. We need people who will have a genuine concern for our well-being and safety.

Psychiatrist R D Laing defined the difference between love and violence in the following way:

> Love and violence, properly speaking, are polar opposites. Love lets the other be, but with affection and concern. Violence attempts to constrain the other's freedom, to force him to act in the way we desire, but with ultimate lack of concern, with indifference to the other's own existence or destiny.
>
> We are effectively destroying ourselves by violence masquerading as love.[18]

As we are recovering from the violence of abuse, the last thing we need is to be surrounded by people who will subject us to further 'violence masquerading as love'. When we surround ourselves with those whose love for us is genuine and unconditional, everything they say and do sends us a different message from the one we received from our abusers. We receive affection, affirmation, care, reassurance, protection, truth, etc. These are the messages that gradually can begin to undo the feelings of badness and uncleanness.

---

[18] R D Laing, *The Politics of Experience and The Bird of Paradise* (London: Penguin, 1990), p.58.

If we are feeling covered in shame and yuck, but there is someone there to speak words of love and affirmation, hold our hands or give us safe hugs with no strings attached, it causes us to doubt in some small way our former belief that we were unworthy of such things. This is especially the case if we have found in ourselves the courage to share with those people the way that we are feeling. The fact that they are still there for us, still loving us unconditionally, even knowing what has happened to us, counteracts the lie that telling our secrets would cause people to hate and reject us.

A higher perspective

Our identity is not only bound up with who we are physically and psychologically. We also recognise a spiritual dimension to our lives. This spiritual dimension to our existence is what connects us with something that is larger, higher and deeper than ourselves. For me and for most of us reading this book, that spiritual dimension is not just a concept but is a God who loves us unconditionally and personally. Moreover, that God has a human face in the person of Jesus. For those of us who know and follow Him, there is something beautiful and profound about the fact that our God became a human being, and was subject to all the pains and sorrows and traumas that we are. He was, as Isaiah puts it:

> a man of sorrows, and acquainted with grief.
> *Isaiah 53:3 (KJV)*

He shares our brokenness and yet, through embracing the very worst of suffering, He models and imparts His wholeness to us. As we allow Him to love and uphold us we come gradually to understand that He is our deepest, truest identity, and He is the One who transforms our lives so that we are restored to the identity God always intended for us – made in His image and likeness.

For those who do not have a personal knowledge of Christ, this spiritual dimension to identity may feel less defined, but it is still a reality. Even those who do not have a full understanding of or belief in God have a sense of what Alcoholics Anonymous and other twelve-step programmes call a Higher Power. However we understand things at this point on our journey, we need to find a way to connect our identity to the spiritual source and ground of our being. Without such a life-giving and sustaining connection, our journey of healing and recovery from childhood abuse will lack something essential, even if we don't fully know what that is.

I don't want to suggest that those who have no clear connection to God cannot find healing. There is much emotional and psychological healing available to any survivor willing to embrace their own recovery. Rather it is the acknowledgement that all the emotional and psychological healing in the world can do little to strike at the core of the shame that is our deepest wound. Shame is an injury that goes deeper than our emotions and our psychological processes, and is in fact about the very core of who we are. Only connecting with something deeper or higher than ourselves can open up the possibility of fully transforming our shame.

Spiritual faith in a sense is all about attempting to deal with the essential badness in us. Pretty much every faith tradition claims to have a way to help those who feel unclean to become clean. The reality is that many of the solutions offered by religions and faith traditions are only partial. Even for those of us who love and follow Jesus, unless we and those around us have really embraced the real good news, the solutions will only be partial. This is because only the real good news holds out any hope to us. Beyond all the shame and other injuries caused by the abuse we suffered, our true self is made in the image and likeness of God (see Genesis 1:27), even if in the stresses and strains of life we have forgotten that fact. In our innermost being, despite our brokenness, pain, shame and distress, we still reflect a divine identity and reality.[19] This is of course the exact opposite of the way that many survivors feel about themselves. It is the exact opposite of what they were told by those who abused them. This is one reason why a strong and authentic spiritual connection is such a powerful force for healing. We may find it hard to feel that positive about ourselves, but when we have a strong heart-to-heart connection with the Creator and source of life, we know that there is a higher perspective. In the eyes of God, we are already loved and accepted unconditionally. Whatever has happened to us, God does

---

[19] This view that our fallen human nature coexists with the image of God in us was held by many of the early Church fathers such as St Gregory of Nyssa (c 335–395) and John Cassian (c 360–435). More recently it is also reflected in the work of theologians such as Karl Barth (1886–1968), T F Torrance (1913–2007) and Dr C Baxter Kruger (https://www.perichoresis.org/, accessed 3rd June 2019).

not see any shame or yuck on us. Furthermore, He has given us the means, through the finished work of Christ, to deal with our own false perception of our essential badness and separation from Him. We may doubt our own sense of self. We may doubt the words and affirmation offered by those who do indeed value and love us. If, however, we can feel His heart for us it may be harder to doubt the unconditional love and affirmation of God.

Of course, our relationship with God may not be straightforward either. Too many of us were brought up with an idea of God that reflected some of the worst aspects of those who abused us. We may have come to believe that He is distant, uncaring and judgemental. We may have come to believe that He punishes us harshly when we cannot live up to some arbitrary rules or standard of goodness. I have worked with many survivors whose concept of God closely mirrored their concept of their own abusive parents. Clearly this sort of spirituality, which institutionalises a form of spiritual abuse, is not going to do us much good in terms of helping us to overcome our sense of innate badness and shame.

We cannot prescribe forms of spirituality for one another, and in this book I am not attempting to convert anyone or promote a particular version of faith. There is a sense in which our spiritual journeys are unique to each of us, and no one can dictate how others should walk their path. My own experience is that Jesus has been the perfect model of love, wholeness, integration and peace. My relationship with Him has been integral both to my own journey of healing and recovery, and in enabling and empowering me to help other survivors of trauma and abuse.

On the slightly less positive side, not all of those people and institutions who use the name of Jesus actually reflect His nature and character. The Christian faith in my experience contains just as many abusive people and organisations as any other faith or social group. Nevertheless, those aberrant versions of faith do not negate the fact that, behind all of our human-made structures and pet dogmas, there is something real and authentic to be found. The Christ. The perfect manifestation of His Father, who is unconditionally loving and affirming of us. Who views us as essentially good and whole, and reflecting the divine nature. Who understands our brokenness and the wounds we carry. Who meets us in our pain and distress, without judging or shaming us. Who does not require us to behave in certain ways, or reach certain standards to be worthy of love and belonging.

Survivor Resources: Simple prayer

There are times when I feel covered in shame. I feel ashamed by what has been done to me, and by how I have responded, even though that shame does not rightly belong to me, but to those who hurt and abused me.

There are times when the burden of that shame weighs so heavily that I don't know how I can possibly keep on going. At these times I struggle to connect with God. I may even question his existence. I find it hard to believe that He can possibly love me.

Even though I want to connect with Him, I don't have the words to pray eloquent prayers or even to feel as if I am making much sense to Him.

At these moments I just want a way to be with Him and to know that He is with me no matter how inadequate, vulnerable or ashamed I feel.

So I sit, in silence, attentive and waiting. I feel my breath moving in and out of my lungs, believing that He breathes with me – His breath, the Holy Spirit continually renewing His life within me.

As I breathe with Him, I call to mind a few simple, ancient words of a prayer that has been prayed for centuries by the Fathers and Mothers in the earliest days of the Church. They went out into the desert to find a quiet space to meet with Him. I sit in whatever quiet space I can find, in my own desert place with Him.

As I breathe in from my belly, I hear in my mind, 'Lord Jesus Christ,' and as I breathe out, I hear, 'Son of God, have mercy.'

Sometimes as I pray, I become distracted and the cares of life and the feelings of pain and distress come over me again. When I realise, I am kind to myself. Without any sense of recrimination I gently bring my attention back to the sensation of my breath, and the words of the prayer, 'Lord Jesus Christ, Son of God, have mercy.'

That's it. That's all I have, this little Jesus prayer that is like a rope in the middle of heavy seas. I hold on to that rope, and recognise that He is holding on to the other end – my anchor while the storm rages.

Sometimes I pray it every day, for fifteen, twenty or thirty minutes, setting a timer on my phone to make sure

I'm not late for the next thing on my schedule. Other days I can barely manage five minutes, or perhaps it is only a few seconds when I am feeling overwhelmed by pain and distress. But whether I pray for a short time or a long time, I know that this simple declaration of faith and cry for mercy from the One who is love itself opens my heart to Him again, when everything else has closed me down.

It seems so simple. Perhaps even too simple. But when I am able to breathe with Him, say His name, call Him Lord and acknowledge my need of Him, I sense His smile of affirmation and love.

Lord Jesus Christ,

Son of God, have mercy.

Supporter's Pause for Thought: Jesus never shames

Jesus is the antithesis of shame. He never shames those who walk with Him or those who come to Him for healing. It doesn't matter who they are, what they have done, or how 'sinful' or 'unclean' the religious may see them as being. Jesus meets them all exactly where they are at, and He treats them with love, dignity and honour. He doesn't even shame the religious authorities and the Pharisees – though He does hold up a mirror that reflects their attitudes back to them. He doesn't shame the one who was to deny him three times, or the disciples who ran away from Gethsemane. He doesn't even shame the one who betrayed Him. As His last service to those whom He loves, He washes the dirt from their feet... all of their feet, including those of Judas Iscariot.

You are called to walk with survivors who have been wounded by abuse and who feel utterly contaminated by what was done to them. You are called to come alongside those who can only react out of their pain, distress and shame. What does it mean to wash their feet? What does it mean to show them the unconditional love and affirmation of the One who is both a man of sorrows broken on a cross and the One who is risen and seated in glory?

Sometimes as you support survivors they will tell you things that either cause them to feel shame, or which may shock you. How you respond at those moments is vital. It has to be non-judgemental and at the same time authentic. The tension between those two can be quite challenging.

Here are ten possible responses for you to think about, pray about and perhaps modify as needed to make them your own. When they feel like a reflection of your heart, give them a try where appropriate.

- When I look at you, I don't see any uncleanness.
- May I give you a hug? Would it be OK to hold your hand gently? (Always ask permission. Never assume.)
- When I touch you/hug you, I don't feel anything unclean or bad.
- This shame and badness doesn't belong to you. It belongs to those who hurt you.
- Whatever they said or did to you, nothing has stuck to you.
- Even though they made you feel bad, it doesn't mean you are bad.

- Those things you do/say/think reflect your pain not your heart, and God sees your heart.

- When you did that it probably felt like the best choice you could make at the time.

- How you see yourself isn't how God sees you. He sees you as good/perfect/beautiful/lovable.

- Jesus has already taken your shame, so you don't need to take it back.

Chapter Eight
Getting Help

Why should we get help?

As survivors it is pretty hard for us to ask for help. For one thing we are not really used to the idea that help might actually be available to us. This was not our experience when we were growing up. Back then there was no one we could trust, so it is hardly surprising that now we are adults it is hard for us to believe that there are people willing to help. Many of us are inclined to try to muddle through on our own. Sometimes we may try to reach out for some help only to find it isn't a good fit for us in some way. Even when we do manage to access the appropriate sort of help, very often we don't really know what to do with it. We tend to map our previous experience on to a new situation.

I recently had a conversation with a survivor I have been working with as a psychotherapist. We had made progress, but possibly not as much as we might have liked. During the course of our conversation we became aware that she did not realise that the process of healing is largely driven by her bringing things to talk about – usually the things that cause the most emotional distress and are hardest to talk about. She had assumed that as the 'adult' in this situation, I would tell her what to talk about, and even what to think, and would give her my solutions to her difficulties. I realised that neither I nor anyone else had ever taken the time properly to explain how therapy works. I had simply assumed that she would know. Of course, the reality is that many survivors were made to hide their distress when they were children, and were threatened and punished if they ever did talk about the things that were happening. They learned back then that what kept them safest was to do exactly what those adults who were abusing them wanted. There was no way she was going to be able to bring the things she needed to talk about until she knew that this was what was expected. More importantly, she needed to know she would not be punished or hurt for talking.

When we have been traumatised and abused as children, and most particularly when that abuse has taken place within our family or at the hands of someone we trusted, we are going to need people who are properly trained and experienced to help us navigate our journey of recovery and healing. Self-help books and well-meaning friends are all helpful as well, of course, but by themselves they are not going to be enough. The life of a survivor is *complicated*, and the path to recovery is similarly not always a simple one. Fortunately, there are people who have the training and the experience to hold a space for us in which we can heal. Typically this space is going to be some form of psychotherapy or counselling, and those who are able to guide us in this place are psychotherapists or counsellors.

This is all well and good. However, the problem for most of us is that the therapeutic space is not like the rest of the world. When we enter it for the first time it is likely to look and feel rather unfamiliar to us. All the rules and norms by which we have lived our lives don't seem to operate in quite the same way. In addition, the relationship we are entering into with our therapist is unlike any other relationship we are likely to have experienced. For one thing it is a professional relationship, with all sorts of boundaries and rules that govern how they as therapists are supposed to relate with us as clients. At the same time, it is an incredibly intimate relationship in which we share things we may never have told another living soul. We have to trust someone – who at least to begin with is a relative stranger – with the key to our broken heart.

For those of us who have been abused as children, this is an almost unthinkable degree of intimacy and trust. Being able to enter this therapeutic space and make the most of everything it has to offer is never going to be easy. But just as we have learned to navigate the world, albeit as 'strangers in a strange land' (Exodus 2:22, KJV), we can also learn to navigate the world of therapy. We can even, because it is such an affirming, empowering and validating world, learn to be more than strangers, and find ourselves thoroughly at home there. In order to be able to do that, however, we need to have a framework to help us understand how that world works and how we can relate to it.

Breaking free of the rules

When we were growing up, like many survivors of childhood abuse we had to live by a rigid set of rules. Some of those rules were explicit, but others were unspoken. Those rules were not neutral or benign. They were set up by our perpetrators – the people who hurt and abused us as children. They were there to make sure we didn't step out of line, that we were kept in the powerless position of being victims. The penalty for breaking those rules was always severe, and in all likelihood constituted further abuse.

Even once we grew up, we still found ourselves living by a version of the abuser's rules. These rules, as long as we allow them to influence us, continue to provide a filter for how we are supposed to feel, think and behave – about ourselves, about our abusers and about the world around us. The abuser's rules continue to keep us powerless and victimised, as long as we choose to live by them.

One of the things that can make it hard for us to understand just how destructive those rules are is that often the abuser's rules are like an extreme and distorted version of the rules the rest of the world lives by. For this reason, it is hard for us as survivors of abuse to rely on the world's rules to show us how to live free of the abuser's rules. What we need is a totally new set of principles to live by, to help us cut through the abuser's rules, and also the less than healthy rules the rest of the world lives by.

There are two ways that we can look at therapy. One way is to see it as a means of helping us to adjust to the world – to find ways to live within the rules and norms of the world around us. However, my personal belief is that this perspective is always going to limit the potential for recovery and healing. We can expect to live a life that is better than we had, but we are still going to find ourselves more affected than most by the limiting and controlling rules the world lives by.

Another, much more radical way to look at therapy is to see it as something transformative, even revolutionary. This view of therapy not only helps us to live free of the effects of the abuse we experienced, but also enables and empowers us to challenge the prevailing culture in which the abusive exercise of power is so normalised, most of us don't even recognise it. In order for us fully to recover and heal, we need to engage in a process that not only changes us, but also has an ongoing impact on the world around us. Looked at from this second perspective, therapy is like a strange upside-down world, in which all the rules about how to live and be are totally different – both from the abuser's rules and to a certain extent from the rules of the world. The rules of this therapy world are the guidelines to recovery. They form a framework for our journey of wholeness and freedom from the things that were done to us, and the core of a new way of living positively in the world as survivors of abuse and agents of transformation.

In the upside-down world of therapy, these are some key guidelines, elements of a framework that is supportive and empowering rather than coercive and restricting. A framework within which survivors can learn to live in wholeness and freedom.

1. What happened was not our fault.
They told us it was our fault. The abusers gave us lots of reasons why we were to blame for the things they did to

us. They did this for reasons that benefited them, and to further disempower us. Primarily they tried to make us believe it was our fault, so that they could feel better about themselves and the horrible things they did. Even abusive people don't want to believe they are doing evil. Sometimes, we still think it might have been our fault. We think they did these things because we were bad or lacking in some way – but that is a lie. It wasn't true then and it isn't true now. It is a revolting, self-justifying lie designed to make us feel even more powerless and worthless than we do already, and to make them feel more powerful and better about themselves.

In therapy we learn that abuse is *never* the fault of the victim. It is always the fault of the abuser. It really is that stark. The one who is abused bears *none* of the responsibility for what happened. The one who abuses is *totally* responsible. There is no excuse for what they did to us. No one, however 'bad' they may have been told they are, deserves to be sexually, physically or emotionally abused. Therefore, there is no way we could possibly have been naughty or bad enough to deserve to be hurt in the ways they hurt us. The things they labelled as naughty or bad, or whatever words they used, were most likely simply the normal behaviour appropriate to any child. Either that, or it was behaviour that was itself generated by the abuse we suffered.

They had everything to gain from the lies they told. Our therapist and our other supporters have nothing to gain from believing we were not to blame. In the light of that, maybe we can start to believe that our therapist and those who love and care for us just might be telling us the truth.

This isn't easy. It represents a huge turnaround in our thinking. Nevertheless, even if it takes a while for us to be fully convinced, we can make a start by consciously choosing to reject the lies the abusers told us.

2. Expressing strong, painful emotions is good.

When we were growing up, it was dangerous for us to express strong, painful emotions. Crying, getting angry or showing distress or fear generally got us into more trouble. We were ridiculed, punished or abused even more. We learned that it was safer to disconnect from our emotions – to stuff them down, hold them in, or detach ourselves from them altogether. Many of us are still doing this today, even when our abusers are no longer present to enforce this rule. Sometimes we believe our emotions are so dangerous they might even hurt other people if we let ourselves show them.

In therapy we are encouraged to be honest about what we are feeling, and to express strong emotions in a way that was never possible before. When we connect with those feelings, we may feel scared and overwhelmed, but even the strongest of feelings eventually pass. When we express them, our therapist and our supporters don't punish us or belittle us. They can cope with our painful feelings no matter how strong they are. Our feelings, even if they are very strong indeed, cannot hurt our therapist, or anyone else.

In fact, the reality is that to make our feelings safe we actually need to find ways to express them. It is as if our mind is like a pressure cooker with soup cooking inside. If we don't have a safety valve to let out the steam, then sooner or later the lid blows off and we end up with soup all over the kitchen. Learning to express our feelings in an appropriate way is that safety valve. Our emotions can't hurt anyone in themselves, not even us, but they can make a mess and cause us problems if we don't find ways to let them out.

3. Remembering and telling the secrets is the key to recovery.

The things that were done to us when we were children were supposed to be kept secret. Our abusers told us we wouldn't be believed. They told us people would laugh at us or hate us. They threatened all sorts of dreadful things would happen if we told anyone or if anyone guessed. Even now it can sometimes be really hard to remember, let alone talk to anyone, about what happened to us. We are scared we won't be believed, that it will make people run away from us, and we are still afraid that we will be punished or hurt worse if we do tell. It is as if the abusers continue to have power over us because we are still keeping their secrets.

In therapy we are encouraged to remember and to speak out the secrets about the abuse we experienced. Remembering the abuse brings it into our conscious awareness where we can process it. Breaking the silence breaks the power of the abuse. It is no longer a horrible toxic secret inside us that we have to carry on our own. Sharing is a bit like vomiting – it's an unpleasant process but it gets the poison out of us. Our therapist is a safe person who is able to hold the things we remember, and hold us while we do the remembering. They believe us; they won't abandon us or laugh at us. They will never use what we tell them to take advantage of us. They will never tell anyone the things we share with them without our permission.

Once we have told someone, and they have treated our secrets with respect and valued us, it may become easier to share with others. If we can tell those who love and care for us, those who support us on our journey, it means we start to feel less alone. It doesn't normalise what was done to us, because there was nothing normal about that, but it does help us to feel not so abnormal about how the abuse has made us feel and respond.

4. We have the resources to survive and recover.

We don't always feel strong, but we are strong. We must have been strong as children not to die or be driven totally crazy by the appalling things the abusers did to us. Even though we felt totally powerless, we must have had some inner resources to survive the things that were happening.

Sometimes now we still feel powerless. But just as we had the resources to survive back then, we have inner resources now. The abusers wanted us to feel weak and powerless, but now things are different. We have people around us who are happy for us to feel strong and powerful. They don't feel threatened when we assert ourselves or draw boundaries.

With the help of our therapist and other supporters, we can start to discover just how strong and powerful we really are. Our strength and power are not like those of the abusers. They were weak people who had to bully and abuse children to feel powerful. Our strength comes from within, from who we were originally created to be. It also comes from others – from the people who love and care about us. Our strength has no need to dominate others. We don't feel the need to pull them down or to hurt them. If anything, we are learning just how much the abuse we experienced has built resilience in us. We are strong and powerful enough to move beyond being a victim. We are strong enough to survive, recover and live a life that is empowered, abundant and free.

5. It is OK to ask questions and check things out.

When we were growing up it was not OK to ask questions of our abusers. If we did, they would most likely punish or take advantage of us. We learned to see them as powerful and ourselves as powerless. We learned that asking questions of the powerful can be a dangerous thing. What took root in us back then was a habit of compliance and obedience, even when that was not in our best interests. Not questioning and not checking things out makes us vulnerable even now to manipulation, exploitation and abuse.

Part of the new learning on our journey of recovery is that asking questions is now a way to stay safe. It is a way of guarding against people who might want to deceive us, control us or persuade us to do things against our own interests. This means that it is absolutely OK for us to ask questions of those who are helping and supporting us. Our therapist, our pastor and other supporters are in positions of great power and influence. They are also sometimes asking us to trust them and to do things that may feel slightly counterintuitive, just because they are different from what we were brought up with. It is totally reasonable for us to ask questions and to try to inform ourselves about what they are doing or saying, and the reasons behind it.

Sometimes we might get worried that our therapist, leaders or supporters could be cross or angry with us. After all, for many of us this is what we were used to. We were often in trouble and punished for it, without even knowing what we had done to make our abusers angry. If we are worried about this, we need to check it out. Our experience growing up and since was that people were not safe, so if we start to worry that our therapist and other supporters may not be as safe as we need them to be, we can ask, knowing that if they really care about us they will not get upset, punish or hurt us in any way. Of course, our therapist and others who are helping us are not perfect – they make mistakes sometimes. They get tired and perhaps may not always be as patient with us as we would like. Sometimes they may say or do something without intending to that triggers us. We need to know that it is safe to tell them, and we need to know that if we do, they will acknowledge whatever has upset us and apologise.

6. Our responses are totally normal and will not destroy us.

Sometimes we get triggered and respond very strongly to things that don't seem to bother other people. This is a totally normal response to the very abnormal things that happened to us when we were children. It doesn't mean that we are mad, stupid, defective or weird. We don't need to be ashamed of our responses. They are there because our mind found ways to protect us at the time from experiencing the full awfulness of what happened. In a sense we can even be grateful that our mind was clever enough to do this. Without it we might well have become overwhelmed or even destroyed by what happened.

However, what it does mean is that now, when we are triggered, we can feel flooded by feelings, memories and physical sensations. It is as if parts of us are experiencing now the things that were happening when we were being abused. The memories can be incredibly vivid. The feelings can be very strong. The physical sensations – sounds, smells, bodily sensations – can feel exactly the same. It can feel as if we are about to be destroyed in some way. But no matter how strong those feelings might be, this is not the case. Though they feel like what happened back then, they are in fact only memories. They are distressing, painful and debilitating, but they will pass. In a little while, the feelings and memories will subside and we will start to feel more settled again. Just as we survived the original experience, we will survive being triggered.

We have tools and techniques to help us to ground ourselves. Some of them may have been given to us by our therapist or counsellor, and there are some in this book. Different tools and techniques suit different people better, but all of them are designed to help us feel less overwhelmed and more in touch with present-day reality. Over time, they will gradually help us to gain strength and build resilience, so we can face the memories and experiences and find ways to process and heal from them.

7. We don't have to censor ourselves.

Being abused meant we could never fully be ourselves. Everything had to be filtered and censored. For some of us we needed to keep our abusers happy in order to try to stop them hurting us even more. For almost all of us we felt we needed to keep what was happening to us, and how it made us feel, a secret.

215

With people who genuinely love and care for us, we shouldn't need to censor ourselves, but sometimes we still do. The fear is that if we don't, if people see who we really are, or hear what has really happened to us and how it makes us feel, they will no longer want to love and care for us. This is one of the reasons why getting proper help can be so important to us. With a good therapist and other supporters who really understand what has happened to us and how it can make us feel, there is no thought or feeling we are not allowed to express. There is nothing that is too shocking, horrible or shameful for them to hear.

We can be free to be fully ourselves, because the therapy space is a safe and healing environment. Those who truly love us and have our best interests at heart won't allow us or help us to do things that physically hurt us, or them, or damage the therapy space. But neither will they use their own discomfort as a reason to limit us or try to keep us quiet about the things we need to share. On this journey of recovery and healing we are free to express ourselves without fear of punishment or withdrawal of love for making mistakes. Whatever we say or do, and however we are, our real supporters will continue to show us unconditional acceptance, care and love.

8. We can make choices.
Those who abused us took away our choices. They were powerful, we were powerless, and we had no option but to do the things they wanted us to. If we tried to make different choices, the likelihood is that we were punished and hurt even more. We learned to live with a sense of our own powerlessness. We felt weak, we felt vulnerable, we felt shamed and degraded. We didn't learn how to make

healthy and appropriate choices for ourselves. This wasn't our fault; we simply never learned that we or what we wanted actually mattered very much. Our choices were always driven by other people, and sometimes by people who chose things that caused us harm. Sometimes we still feel driven to make choices that punish and hurt us in some of the ways that our abusers punished and hurt us.

In the healing space of therapy, we have choices. Who we are and what we want matter. We will never be forced to do anything against our will. We will never be made to do anything that hurts, punishes, shames or degrades us. Sometimes those who support and help us may challenge us when they see us making choices that do any of those things. They won't force us to stop, but they will point out what we are doing and ask the questions that may help us to reconsider. Sometimes our therapist or other supporters may have a strong recommendation about a good course of action for us, but they will not take away our freedom to choose. We can choose to do it even though it feels difficult and scary, or we can decide that we are not ready to do that yet. In the end it is still our choice, and we will not be punished or hurt for doing something different.

Sometimes there will be boundaries and ground rules that our therapist and other supporters have agreed with us. These are intended to help us stay safe and to help us on our journey of healing and recovery. However, these are not forced on us, but are drawn up in agreement with us, and we can ask for them to be reviewed at any time.

9. It is OK to make mistakes.

When we were growing up we may have been punished for making mistakes or for getting something wrong. Some of us were physically and verbally abused. Some of us were humiliated, degraded and shamed when we made a mistake. Some of us were deprived of food, sleep or basic care to punish us for getting something wrong. We lived in constant fear that we would not do things well enough, or be good enough. For many of us, the rules changed and the goalposts moved all the time. We would try as hard as we could to get things right or not to make a mistake, but it was an impossible task. The truth is that for some of us, whatever we did would be wrong, and however we were would not be right.

Some of us learned that we had to try as hard as we could to be perfect and to perform flawlessly. We may still be trying to do that in our lives generally now. Others of us learned that being good enough was simply not possible, because we could never meet the arbitrary and shifting standards of our abusers. We gave up and may still not feel it is worth doing the best we can with things, because we believe we will never be good enough.

On our journey of recovery and healing, we don't have to get everything right. It is OK to find things difficult, to make mistakes or to be unable to do something. Recovery, whether it takes the form of therapy or some other supportive space, is a new way of being for us and it can be hard. It takes time, and sometimes we have to go slowly, learning as we go from mistakes and from the things we find too hard. We will never be punished for falling short. Our therapist and other supporters will be consistent with us. They will not get cross with us if we make mistakes, and they will never reject or abandon us just because we are finding things hard.

10. We are worthy of care and love.

Many of us grew up believing we were not worthy of care or love. We came to believe that all we deserved was abuse, neglect and humiliation. We asked ourselves why, if we were worthy of care and love, did no one love and care for us? Adults abused and humiliated us, so we started to believe that was all we were worth.

For most of us, we have lived a large part of our lives with the belief that we are not worthy, and that we do not deserve to be loved and cared for. We may well have started on our journey of recovery and healing with those same beliefs in place. However, in therapy and in other genuinely supportive settings the message we receive will be different. In fact, it will be the exact opposite. We will be told repeatedly that we are worthy of care and love, not because of anything we do, but simply because we are.

There will be times when that is hard to understand, and even harder to trust. We may find that we keep waiting for the care and love our therapist and other supporters show towards us to turn into something we are more familiar with – abuse, neglect and shame. However, no matter what we say or do, the message remains the same. Within a healing space and the healing relationships that go with it, we are told and shown consistently in many ways that we are accepted, cared for and loved. It may take a long time, but very gradually, if we are able to keep walking on our journey, we will begin to believe that it might be true. We will start to accept that we might just possibly be someone who is worthy of care and love. When we come to believe it fully, we will no longer be victims, or even just survivors. We will be those who, despite our history of abuse, are living free, empowered and abundant lives.

Survivor Resources: Red flags in the people we trust

It isn't always easy for us to know who to trust. We need people who will help and support us, whether they are therapists, family, friends or people from our church communities. Lots of people may say they can help us and want us to trust them, but our hearts are fragile and need looking after.

Here are some red flags to help us decide if the people who say they care for us and that we can trust them are really going to be good for us in the long run. When we start our journey of recovery and healing, we may well struggle with some of these, and not know whether these are genuine feelings or are based in our distorted expectations. However, if after a while too many of these red flags still keep showing up, it may mean we need to take some decisions about whether we continue to allow these people to be close to us and whether they are actually capable of helping us in the long term.

- If they say or do things that make us feel ashamed about our actions, words, feelings or thoughts.
- If they get uncomfortable or try to shut us down when we express strong emotions.
- If they do not treat the things we share with them with respect and keep them confidential.
- If they act in such a way that we feel like we are stupid or not capable.

- If they get cross or refuse to answer when we ask questions or check things out.

- If they make us feel like we are weird or abnormal.

- If we feel like we can't be ourselves, or that there are things we cannot share with them.

- If they don't allow us to make free choices about our lives.

- If they get mad or belittle us when we get things wrong or find stuff difficult.

- If they do not help us to feel that we deserve to be loved and cared for.

Supporter's Pause for Thought: Being family

Creating a healing environment for those who are wounded by abuse is not difficult. It isn't about a particular place, having special things or even about all of the people involved being completely sorted out. It is about helping people to belong.

> God sets the lonely in families.
> *Psalm 68:6*

Recovery from abuse takes place best in the context of a loving and supportive family. Particularly for those whose families were the source of hurt and abuse, you and others like you may be the nearest thing they will ever have to genuine family. It is important to ask yourself some very real questions about what it might mean to take on the role of a surrogate family person for someone who has been abused.

- What does it mean for you to be family to those who have been traumatised and wounded by abuse?

- How are you going to help them to belong, without them feeling they have to behave in certain ways to be worthy of your love and care?

- What are the biggest challenges you are likely to face in doing this?

- What help are you going to need to support you in being family to a survivor? You cannot do this on your own. You will need other people.

- Are there limits on the support you may be able to give them? It's OK if there are, but they need to be clear and out in the open.

- How will you feel if or when they test you, to see if you really care for them in the way you say you do?

- What are the circumstances (if any) under which you might stop being family for a survivor?

Chapter Nine
Healthy Boundaries

Why are boundaries important?

For all of us, healthy boundaries are an important part of how we relate with other people and with the rest of the world. If our boundaries are appropriate and healthy, our relationships with others and with our environment are likely to be healthy. If on the other hand our boundaries are not appropriate or healthy, then our relationships with others and with the world around us are likely to be distorted. Those relationships may not be healthy and life-giving for us, and they may not be healthy and life-giving for others either.

It probably doesn't come as any great surprise to realise that for survivors of abuse, healthy boundaries present something of a challenge. Abuse, by its very nature, represents a gross violation of our boundaries. Limits that should have been respected were not. In fact, as children we were not powerful and strong enough to set boundaries for ourselves, and those who abused us did things that violated our sense of safety and identity. As a result, even though we are now adults and in theory can set boundaries to help us feel safe and secure, we often find it almost impossible. This is particularly the case because the abuse destroyed our sense of what was an OK boundary to have in relation to other people and what was not. For the same reason, there are times when we can also find it hard to recognise the boundaries that others draw – not because we wish to cross the lines or cause a problem, but simply because we have never learned to recognise where the lines are or what they mean. Learning about healthy boundaries is pretty much a vital life skill, but it is also an area in which, as survivors, we are probably going to need to make up some lost ground.

Protecting what is valuable

We need boundaries to protect the things that are valuable to us. If we have a physical object that is valuable – say a piece of jewellery – we protect it with a physical boundary. We put it in a lockable jewellery box, or, if it is valuable enough, we might put it in a safe or even a bank deposit box. If there are things about our lives that we find valuable in less obvious ways, we need to put a different sort of boundary around them in order to protect them. These valuable things can be almost anything. It could be the people that we love and care about. It could be our work. It could be some aspect of our lives that brings us joy. It could even be something less tangible or more abstract such as particular beliefs or values. What makes these things valuable is quite simply that we place value on them. They mean something to us, and we have an emotional connection to and investment in them.

What we sometimes fail to understand, however, is that this value that we attribute either to tangible things, people or abstract ideas doesn't come from nowhere. It has a source, and that source is within us. The ability to place value on things comes from the fact that we ourselves are valuable. We have value, and we need protecting as much as any other valuable object or person. If we don't find ourselves valuable and worthy of protection, the chances are that we will find it difficult to derive value from anything or anyone else. We might for example value another person as a friend, but if we don't value ourselves, we will find it difficult to protect and nurture our relationship with them in healthy and appropriate ways.

Loving and following Jesus, if we understand it correctly, means that we know our value is a given. It always was something intrinsic to us as created beings, made in the image of an infinitely valuable God. However, the problem for us as survivors of abuse is that the trauma has disconnected us from our own value and our own identity. We have come to believe either that the abuse has devalued us, or that the abuse only happened because we have no value. These beliefs are powerful for us because they contain a grain of truth among all the lies and deception. The deceptive message that is sent by abusers is that we were not valuable to them. Had we been valuable they would not have done these terrible things to us. Perhaps even worse is the version of the lie that tells us our only value came from the fact that we did the things they wanted us to, and were able to keep them happy. Added to these lies, the sense of powerlessness and shame that came with the abuse we experienced causes us to feel even further devalued and worthless. We have been subtly drawn into a view of ourselves that says we weren't valuable enough to be protected from abuse. As a result, the abuse we suffered stripped us of what little value we did feel we had.

The fact that these are false beliefs doesn't make them any less powerful, and the fact that all too often we don't see ourselves as valuable makes it very difficult for us to put genuine value on the important things in our lives. This has a knock-on effect. What we don't value, we don't protect or nurture. As survivors of abuse, we very often fail to protect and nurture ourselves and the important things in our lives. That lack of protection means that we do not draw appropriate and effective boundaries for ourselves – not only because we don't know how, but because we don't value ourselves enough.

As is so often the case with our journey of recovery and healing, we face something of a chicken-and-egg situation. In a normal, non-abusive childhood, we would have learned to value the important things in our lives and to draw boundaries to protect them, because we would have started from a place of valuing ourselves. However, because our childhood was broken by abuse, we cannot start learning to draw boundaries where we would have started. We have to work in a way that may seem a bit backward. One of the things that is a kind of testament to the resilience of survivors is that almost always we can find things, whether tangible or intangible, that are important to us – things to value, despite the fact that we don't value ourselves. I have worked with many survivors who had little or no value for themselves, but were able to find value in a pet animal, or something similar. This is a good place to start. As we begin to identify the things in our lives that we do value, we are able to learn to protect them with appropriate boundaries. In doing this, we begin to learn something important at an unconscious level. We begin to learn that the things we value are actually partial reflections of the things that are valuable in ourselves. Gradually, as we learn to value and protect these things, we find ourselves more able to value the core of who we are.

In the survivor resources at the end of this chapter, there is an exercise in learning to protect and nurture our core values. These are expressions of who we are, and they say something about our identity that defies our broken self-image. They also say something about our destiny. Destiny may seem like an old-fashioned sort of word, but just as each one of us has value in who we are, we also have value in what we do. For many survivors, both of these may feel out of reach. Our common experience is not simply that we have no worth, but also that what we do has no worth. Sometimes we see ourselves as nothing, and the things we do as worthless failures. However, these beliefs are untrue. The reality is that every single one of us has a unique, created, core identity – who we were born to be, even if we don't yet know who that is. Just as we have a core identity, we also have a destiny that flows out of who we were born to be. This is what we were born to do, the purpose for which we were created. Of course, we may not yet know what our destiny is either. Nevertheless, as we pursue our recovery, we can begin to discover who we really are and to pursue what we were born to do.

Defining limits

We also need boundaries to define limits for us. This is not necessarily a restrictive thing. In fact, if the boundaries are appropriate and healthy, they are the very opposite of restrictive. On the contrary, they are actually incredibly liberating. This is because every boundary actually helps to define two things, which are like the two sides of the same coin.

Firstly, boundaries define the area within which we have freedom to act. If we try to think about it as being a little like living in a house with a garden, the garden is surrounded by a fence or a wall, which forms the boundary around our property. Within that boundary, we have freedom to act in whatever ways suit us, providing we are not infringing on the boundaries of other people. So if we want to mow our lawn into crazy zigzag stripes and paint our front door lime green, no one is able to stop us. Even if others don't appreciate or approve of our good taste and are rude enough to say so, we don't have to take any notice. On the other hand, if we want to play thrash metal music at high volume in the small hours of the morning, that has an impact outside the boundaries of our property. We may be infringing the boundaries of others. They can (and probably will) tell us to stop, and if we don't do so, they might use the law to compel us.

Secondly, boundaries define our area of responsibility. Using the same metaphor of a house and garden, we are responsible for what happens inside the boundaries of our property. If the postperson comes onto our property to deliver mail, and as they walk up the garden path towards the front door they are attacked by the feral pet llama we keep in the garden, we are responsible for any injuries done to them. The postperson is, implicitly at least, there with our permission and so we are responsible for their safety. We have the freedom to keep a feral pet llama, but we are responsible within our boundary for making sure the feral ruminant doesn't decide to chew on anyone. However, we are not responsible for what might happen to the hapless postperson when they go next door or even what happens in the street outside our home. If the postperson is savaged by next door's sabre-toothed tiger, or is abducted by aliens in the street, we cannot be held responsible.

In all seriousness, the point is that boundaries empower us. When we were abused, we were disempowered. Anything that helps us to take power back for ourselves is something we need to learn as part of our recovery. Boundaries empower us to know what we are and are not responsible for. Our abusers tried to make us responsible for their actions and the consequences. But we were never responsible for what they did. They violated our boundaries and, by doing so, took away both our freedom and our power. By learning to re-establish our boundaries in a healthy and appropriate way, we learn not to take responsibility for the things that do not belong to us. In learning to take responsibility for what is rightfully ours, but nothing more, we find the freedom and power to take action.

In a very practical sense, we were not responsible for the abuse, and we are not responsible for the pain and the distress it has caused in our lives. However, we do carry some responsibility for what we do with those things now.

It may not seem fair, but the reality is that no one else is responsible for our recovery. No one else can walk that journey for us, and no one else can be responsible for our healing. We may not have had any choice about what happened to us, but we do have a choice about whether and how we embrace our recovery. We can invite others to help us along the way, and we may find that people are willing to be with us and walk with us on the journey. They could be friends, loved ones or professional helpers such as therapists, but no matter how much they are willing to accompany us and give us their love, care, support, wisdom and experience, we are still the ones responsible for our own healing journey.

Developing relationships

We also need boundaries to help us develop healthy and appropriate relationships. This is because boundaries by their nature are inherently relational. They help us to define where we stand in relation to other people. They help us work out how we can connect with them in healthy ways, and how we can maintain appropriate distance and separation from them.

The way our boundaries develop mirrors the way in which we develop as children. The first stage of our developmental journey takes us from dependence to independence. As babies and small children, we are completely dependent on our parents – most especially our mothers. In fact, for nine months our boundaries are completely contained within hers. Even after we are born, we are so dependent on our mothers and on other caregivers that although we are no longer physically contained within our mother, we are emotionally and psychologically merged with her, at least for the first few months of life.

Over time we gradually develop an identity that is separate from our mother or other caregivers. At the same time our boundaries begin to develop separately from those of our parents. The more we grow, the more distinct our boundaries and our identity become. In a healthy developmental process, we reach adulthood with our boundaries and our identities whole and distinct from those of our parents.

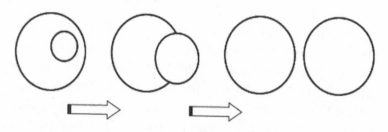

Diagram 1: Dependence to independence

The second stage of the journey takes us from independence to interdependence. In healthy development this stage runs to some extent parallel with the first, though if we have not experienced good boundaries when growing up, this development often does not happen until later on in life.

This stage of the journey represents our growing social interaction with others. As we develop independence from parents, we simultaneously develop mutual interaction with other people. Where our boundaries with those other people are appropriate, our identity develops further in community and family. It also reflects the perfect mutual interdependence of the three persons of the Trinity.

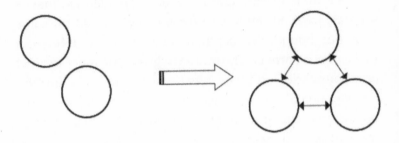

Diagram 2: Independence to interdependence

Healthy personal boundaries are essentially connected with our sense of self-worth. However, as we know, traumatic experiences in childhood damage our sense of self. This is particularly so for those of us who have been abused as children. Our experience is of boundaries consistently and devastatingly ignored and overridden. Therefore, as survivors we tend to be left with a very distorted and depleted sense of our own self-worth – it is not surprising then that we will tend to find it more challenging to draw and maintain healthy boundaries. In fact, many of the long-term problems faced by survivors are connected with the difficulties we find in drawing and keeping healthy boundaries. With some mental health issues associated with trauma, the inability to keep consistent, appropriate boundaries is one of the criteria that can lead to our being labelled in that way.

It is very hard for us when we have a damaged sense of self-worth to draw and maintain healthy boundaries. At the same time, if we are not able to do this in an effective way, it is very hard for us to build up any sense of self-worth. Fortunately, healthy boundaries can be taught. There is a clear process which can be learned by anyone – including us. This is especially important for us as survivors, because learning to draw healthy boundaries can help provide us with a 'here and now' framework within which our sense of self-worth can begin to recover and become whole.

Identifying boundary issues

When we grow up with our boundaries being violated by abuse, or if healthy boundaries were not modelled for us, it will almost inevitably lead to us having boundary issues as adults. These boundary issues represent a filter through which we relate with the world and with others. In order to learn how to draw and maintain healthy boundaries for ourselves, we need to understand the particular boundary issues we face.

We need to begin by addressing the common misconception that there is only one way in which we can have inappropriate boundaries. In fact, there are four main types of issue we can have with developing and maintaining healthy boundaries. Essentially these represent the positions we take up, or the less than healthy strategies that we habitually use in relating with other people. It's probably fair to say at this point that pretty much everyone will use at least one of these strategies at some time or another. None of us had a perfect upbringing, and as a result none of us has developed perfect boundary-setting skills. However, for those of us who are survivors of abuse, some of these strategies have become ingrained, and we find ourselves regularly tripping over at least one, if not more, of the boundary issues we are going to look at.

It is probably worth mentioning at this point that although some people may have one predominant boundary position that they take up, most will also adopt one or more of the other strategies. It is also important that we do not fall into the trap of feeling bad about our habitual boundary issues. We learned these strategies from childhood. At the time they were the best options we had in order to help us stay safe, and in many ways they have at times served us well. In fact, we have learned them so effectively that they have become established in our unconscious minds. Until our attention is drawn to them, we will mostly be unaware of how they are making us behave in relation to our own and other people's boundaries.

Table 1 is a diagram to help us understand the four different types of boundary issues.

Victim

The reality is that most of us who were abused in childhood will take up the victim position from time to time. This is hardly surprising given that we were victimised in some appalling ways. Our boundaries were overridden with devastating consequences, and as a result we find it incredibly hard to set anything like a clear and appropriate boundary. To put it another way, we find it hard to say no, or at least to say no in a way that others will listen to and respect. This means that in many ways we are still vulnerable to other people. We are easily manipulated into doing things we don't really want to be doing. We

	Doesn't Say	Doesn't Hear
No	**Victim** *Doesn't **set** boundaries*	**Trespasser** *Doesn't **see** boundaries*
Yes	**Absentee** *Sets boundaries against **providing** help*	**Martyr** *Sets boundaries against **receiving** help*

Table 1: Boundary issues

often find our actions being controlled by others, and also by our own inability to draw a clear boundary or say a clear 'no'. We may even continue to find ourselves in situations where we are abused, even though we are now grown-ups.

For some of us, we may be abused in similar ways to the abuse we experienced as children. For others of us, the abuse may be more subtle or different in some ways. I know for myself that after the abuse that I experienced both within and outside my family, I continued to find myself in a victim position, particularly with people in authority such as bosses and managers. However, not all of the particulars of the abuse I experienced as a child were replicated. For the most part I found myself subjected to a great deal of manipulation and control, which sometimes crossed the line into outright bullying in the workplace.

As well as the more obvious ways in which our victim boundary issues can show themselves, we may find ourselves in the victim position in some less obvious ways. For example, we may as adults tend to be quite needy and dependent, always looking for someone we perceive as stronger than ourselves to take responsibility for us and our lives, or possibly to rescue us from whatever situation we may find ourselves in.

Trespasser

Trespasser is the boundary position most often associated not with survivors, but with those who abused us. They violated our boundaries and trespassed on areas of our lives that they had no right to access. Trespassers do not see or respect the boundaries set by others. If victims are unable to say a clear and effective 'no', then trespassers are unable to hear or respect when someone tries to say 'no'. It is probably fairly obvious to say that trespassers tend to be manipulative, controlling and at least potentially abusive. However, there are some less comfortable things we may need to face up to about those with trespasser boundary issues.

The first is that we, ourselves, may be trespassers. Not in the sense that we are sometimes afraid of – that we ourselves might become like those who abused us. The reality is that although that can happen, the vast majority of survivors of abuse do not themselves become perpetrators. Nevertheless, we can still be trespassers in other ways. Our experience as survivors was that we did not have our boundaries respected – our 'no' was not heard or was not effective. Because our own boundaries were not recognised or respected, we may well not have learned to recognise or fully respect the boundaries of others. This doesn't mean we are abusive, but it may mean that we could unintentionally be somewhat controlling or manipulative at times. This should not surprise us too much, and once again we need to have some self-compassion about it. Our experience as children was of having nothing in the way of power or control, even over our own bodies and minds. It is totally understandable that we may unconsciously try to regain power and control in order to make ourselves and our environment feel safe and predictable.

The second thing we may need to come to terms with is that sometimes when we think we are helping people, we may actually be controlling and manipulative in some subtle ways. The need to protect, rescue or fix others can actually be a way in which we try to feel in control of a situation, at the expense of trespassing on someone else's area of responsibility. This is just as true if we are in an active helping role with others, as well as just being one of the ways in which we relate to other people. When we trespass in this way, we can find ourselves giving input where it isn't asked for, and also we can find that we are actually enabling someone to avoid taking responsibility for themselves and their own issues. For those of us who are both survivors and professional helpers, this can be quite a hard thing to have to grasp. We want to help, particularly if we identify with the story of those we are helping, but rescuing and fixing people will in the long run prove to be counterproductive.

I sometimes tell a silly story to illustrate this point. One day, when I had actually been running some training on boundaries(!), my wife and I were invited out to dinner with friends in the evening. We came to the end of the meal, and there was a lovely cheese platter put in front of us, on which was an entire wheel of Brie cheese. My wife asked our hostess how she would like the Brie cut, in slices or wedges, and our hostess said she would prefer wedges. I watched as my wife, slightly distracted by the conversation, started to cut a slice from the edge of the cheese. I said, 'No! She said she wanted wedges.' My wife gave me the look that said without words, *We're going to talk about this later.* After we got home, she was really quite cross with me, saying that I had shown her up in front of our friends. I protested that I had only been trying to save her from making a mistake and possibly irritating our hostess. What she said next made me realise I had trespassed on her boundary. 'If I make a mistake, I'll take responsibility for it. I'm an adult, not a child. It's not your responsibility to protect me or put me right.'

As a survivor who is now in a helping role with other survivors, I have come to realise that I need to guard against over-responsibility, and therefore trespassing on the boundaries of those I am working with.

Absentee

The absentee style of boundary issue takes us into new territory. The previous types of boundary issue have all been around being able to say 'no' or to recognise a 'no'. When we have absentee as a style of boundary issue, the difficulties are not around *no* at all, but around *yes*. The absentee sets a boundary, and quite often a strong boundary, but it isn't an appropriate or helpful one. Instead it is a boundary against providing help and support, or being emotionally available to other people. In other words, the absentee doesn't say *yes*.

Those of us with absentee issues may well have grown up in families that were emotionally not expressive. There were most likely many strong emotions present, but they were not acknowledged or dealt with in helpful or appropriate ways. We may well have experienced high levels of pain and distress, but the culture within our family was to ignore it or to pretend it wasn't happening. When we expressed those feelings, the chances are that our distress was ignored at best, or we may even have been mocked or belittled for showing our pain. As a result, we never learned how to deal with the strong emotions of others, or more importantly, of ourselves. The irony is that we may in fact be highly sensitive to the pain of others; we may feel it and identify with it all too easily. Our fear is that we will be drawn into their distress and may become overwhelmed, because we never had the opportunity to develop ways of dealing with high levels of distress in helpful ways.

Therefore, we tend to absent ourselves emotionally and even physically when faced with the needs of others. We find excuses not to be present or not to offer help. At times we may even fail to see that there is a need at all. We aren't simply being selfish here. Again, this is a self-protective strategy. The unconscious belief is that what we fail to notice can't hurt us. Of course, this belief isn't true. In our original families, those unacknowledged and unexpressed emotions were powerful, and because they had no acceptable outlet, they were also highly damaging. Strong emotions repressed into the unconscious almost always become toxic, and ultimately can in themselves become the drivers for further abuse, compounding the trauma we have already experienced.

It is also possible for those of us who are helping survivors to adopt an absentee role. This is especially likely to be true when we feel overwhelmed by the issues or the feelings of the person we are helping. In effect we may end up mirroring the strategies for dealing with feelings that were present in our own families. As a result, we may find ourselves unconsciously avoiding engaging with the issues and the feelings. Indeed, we may find ourselves avoiding engaging with the person we are helping at all in anything other than a superficial way. We may also, as helpers and supporters, become drawn into mirroring the experience of those we are helping, and unconsciously replicating the emotionally unavailable strategies of their birth families.

Unfortunately, this sort of dynamic can be quite common among those helping survivors of abuse, such as therapists and others. It is too easy for us, if we don't have some understanding of why we are wanting to put an emotional distance between ourselves and those we are trying to help, to put emotional barriers in place, and to justify it in the name of having 'good boundaries'. Of course, it is true that as helpers we do need to have good and appropriate boundaries, but it is unhelpful to survivors of abuse if we hide behind an absentee strategy.

Martyr

Those of us who adopt the martyr style when dealing with boundaries find it difficult or impossible to receive help from others. We tend to feel that we are the only ones who can be trusted to do the things that need doing, even when we are completely overwhelmed by all that we have to do. Often we feel isolated, unloved, uncared for and unsupported. Though if we are true martyrs, we wouldn't dream of letting anyone know we feel any of this. We just carry on doing everything and pretending not to mind. It is important to understand that there may in fact be plenty of help on offer. The problem is that we either do not hear or cannot trust that the 'yes' we hear from others is genuine. Even if it is genuine, we are afraid that it may not be adequate. When we are martyrs, we also tend to be perfectionists. Very often we have the unconscious belief that no one can do things quite as well as we can.

Sometimes our martyr boundaries are obvious – we simply do not ask or do not accept the help that is on offer from others. At other times the barriers we put in place to receiving help may be a bit more subtle. We may say that we want help, and we may express gratitude for the help that is on offer to us, but it doesn't necessarily mean we are actually going to accept it when the time comes to do so. This is a strategy born out of fear and the need to remain in control. As survivors we find it incredibly hard to trust. We were probably let down badly as children by those who were supposed to love, care for and protect us. In some ways there is little incentive for us to trust that the help we are offered now is genuine or enough. This difficulty in trusting extends to how we relate with those who are helping us on our journey of recovery and healing. One of the founders of Transactional Analysis, Eric Berne, identified one of the ways in which martyrs put up barriers to receiving help. He called it the 'Why don't you–Yes, but' game.[20] In this unconscious, habitual defensive game, when we have help offered to us, we will find some legitimate-sounding reason why we can't accept it, or why it isn't quite right for our needs. It all sounds very reasonable, because of course we need to get the right sort of help. The reality is, however, that often with some creative thinking, we might actually be able to overcome our doubts and get what we need, but that is not really what we are trying to do. In fact, we are trying to keep the possibility of further harm or distress away from us by putting up barriers, because receiving help feels just too risky.

As always when looking at these types of issues, we need to practise self-compassion. We were badly hurt as children, and the impulse to protect ourselves is a perfectly natural one. Many of us also grew up in an environment in which we had to take on adult or carer roles as children. This may have been as a result of genuine care needs on the part of the adults in our lives, or it may have been because the abuse we experienced forced us into taking adult roles. Either way, the help, support and care we needed was not available to us back then, and we find it very hard to believe that it is going to be available to us now.

Impact of boundary issues

For survivors, the biggest impact of boundary issues is usually going to be on relationships. In a sense, abuse is the

---

[20] Eric Berne, *Games People Play: The Basic Handbook of Transactional Analysis* (New York: Ballantine Books, 1964).

ultimate relational poison, as it distorts our view of what relationships could and should look like. But as we will see in more detail in the next chapter, human beings are created to be relational beings. When we are children, we have relational needs that mean we have to be dependent on others. It is this need for relationship that can easily become distorted when our boundary styles are driven by the abuse we experienced.

On the one hand, there is a danger that we could begin to form *co-dependent* relationships. Co-dependence, as its name suggests, involves a situation in which two people with dependence needs come together. If we form a friendship or any other relationship with someone who like ourselves has high dependence needs, it is likely that we will come to support or enable one another in our boundary issues. Either we enable one another in not setting appropriate boundaries, or alternatively we may enable one another in actually violating one another's boundaries. One common example of this might be when we have a partner who is alcoholic or drug-addicted, but we ourselves are not. If we are in a co-dependent relationship, it is quite likely either that we will not recognise the signs of their dependent drinking or drug use, or if we do recognise it, we may tolerate the destructive and toxic effects of their addiction. We may even do things to enable their addiction, such as making sure always to buy alcohol for them or arranging our lives in such a way that they can easily sleep off a hangover. It is not uncommon for marriages or other partnerships of this sort to remain apparently stable for years, until the addicted partner gives up drinking or drug use. At that point the relationship often falls apart, because the non-addicted partner actually needed the other person to be dependent on them.

On the other hand, there is also a danger that we could become *isolates*. Isolation is rooted in a lack of trust. Because the abuse we experienced was such a betrayal of trust, we begin to adopt the belief that various groups, and the community as a whole, are not to be trusted. We feel we don't fit or don't quite belong. Typically, we will often find ourselves on the fringes of any social group, never really feeling accepted or acceptable. Part of the problem is that these isolating beliefs tend to become self-fulfilling prophecies. We don't feel we belong, and so we often don't develop or bother to exercise the social skills needed to fit in. This isn't us being consciously awkward. Rather it is our trying unconsciously to protect ourselves from feeling hurt, rejected or abandoned by others. Of course, this process goes two ways. The others in social groupings tend to pick up, at least unconsciously, that we see ourselves as outsiders, and equally unconsciously they may well respond in kind. Our worst fears are realised and we become ever more deeply embedded in a position of social isolation.

Survivor Resources: Protecting our value

We may have many things that we find valuable in our lives. But as survivors there are certain core values that others probably take for granted, but which for us were almost certainly compromised by the abuse we experienced.

In this exercise, we are going to identify these three core values and ask ourselves a series of questions that may give us an idea about how to protect them – that is, how to draw healthy and appropriate boundaries.

Truth

As survivors we need to know that we are being told the truth. We need to know that people, things and situations are as they appear to be and are not suddenly going to change into something else.

Safety

As survivors we value safety almost above all else. If a person or a situation isn't safe, our experience is that it can have disastrous consequences. We become triggered because we are suddenly faced with people and situations that for whatever reason do not feel safe, even if there is no actual threat.

Connection

As survivors we need connection. Even if we don't believe we do, we cannot make the journey of recovery and healing on our own. Our ability to connect in healthy and appropriate ways was compromised by the abuse, so we need to find ways to connect now that are not going to threaten our well-being and stability.

Boundary questions

For each of the core values above, we try to ask ourselves the following questions:

1. Why is this value important to me?

2. What does it mean to me for this value to be protected and nurtured? Think of some practical examples.

3. What signals to me that this value is protected and that all is well?

4. What signals to me that this value may be under threat? This could be an emotion or a physical feeling (eg a discomfort in the body).

5. What decisions and/or actions do I need to take to protect and nurture this value?

6. How am I going to communicate these decisions and who needs to know about them?

7. If the decisions and actions I take form a boundary, under what circumstances might I let another person inside and who might that be?

8. Who do I need to get to help me to maintain my boundaries and stick with my decisions?

9. When am I going to review the decisions and actions I have taken to set these boundaries, and with whom?

10. What other values are important to me, that I might want to ask these questions about?

Remember, your answers to these questions are not set in stone. Neither do they have to be perfect. They are a work in progress, something to keep under review. As we grow and heal from the abuse we experienced, it may be that we want to draw different boundaries, or to refine the ones we have.

Supporter's Pause for Thought: What about our own boundaries?

It is easy for those who are supporting survivors to look at them and make pronouncements about their need for appropriate boundaries. But what about the boundaries of those who are helping, and those who are leading the churches in which survivors are hoping to find loving family and community? Here are some things for you to watch out for when you are supporting survivors of abuse: things that point to boundary issues – not in them, but in you.

- If you are struggling with your own unresolved pain, are your victim issues going to cause you to ignore your own needs and those of your loved ones, because you are too busy giving out to those you are supporting? It is important to give and support selflessly, but there needs to be a balance, otherwise you will burn out and your family life will suffer.

- Is the help you give always wanted and needed? It is possible to trespass on the boundaries of survivors without meaning to. If your help and support cause them to feel less empowered and less able to grow and heal, it's time to re-evaluate whether what you are doing is really in their best interests.

- Do you find yourself going emotionally cold or disconnecting from the survivors you are supporting? Do you resent the time and the energy they take from you and from other things, and find excuses not to be available? Perhaps it is time to ask yourself what it is about their experience and their distress that makes you so uncomfortable.

- Do you sometimes feel that you are the only person who really understands the ones you are trying to help and support? Do you feel that what others offer them is not relevant or even counterproductive? Do you turn away the offers of help given by others, because you don't want them to mess up the vital work you are doing? Do you secretly believe that you are called to save them? Perhaps it is time to take a step back, and ask those around you whose judgement you respect to give you their wisdom and their perspective. After all there is only one Saviour, and you are not Him!

Chapter Ten
Relational Restoration

How abuse messes up relationships

The young man sitting in front of me was physically and sexually abused as a child, by his father and later by a teacher at boarding school. He seems very confident, even slightly aggressive, but as we get below the surface he talks about how inadequate he feels in his close relationships. He is in his mid-thirties, and his marriage is in trouble. Despite the fact that he and his wife have known and dated each other since they were both teenagers at the church youth group, he has never felt as if he was good enough for her.

'I'm petrified she's going to leave me,' he says. 'I'm such a loser. Really she should give me the push.'

In a halting voice, he confesses that from the earliest days of their marriage he has been unfaithful to her. When life gets too stressful, he goes out, telling her that he is with friends, but actually he goes alone to pubs and clubs, and drinks until any inhibitions disappear. Then he seeks out casual encounters, with prostitutes or on online dating apps.

'I don't care about them,' he tells me. 'They don't mean anything. I just have sex and then I'm gone. No emotional

investment at all. I feel horrible about myself afterwards, but for some reason I don't feel as scared that my wife is going to leave me... for a while at least.'

Being abused as children can put our subsequent relationships under pressure. Because of the betrayal of trust, our ability to make and sustain healthy relationships, whether they are social, professional or intimate, can all too often end up proving to be something of a minefield. Just when we think it's all going OK, we find ourselves tripping over something and it all blows up in our face.

Like all human beings we are wired for relationship. It isn't something we learn; it is something we are born with. Something in our DNA knows that in order to survive and to live life to the full we have to be in relationship with others, even if we have different styles of relating. For example, those of us who are introverts are not, as some people may think, antisocial or not interested in relationships. We still need friends and family, but relate to them in a different way from those of us who are extroverts. We are wired for relationship, but when we are abused as children, the trauma we experience is at least partly *relational* in nature.

If we were abused by people within our immediate family, it means that our bond with them, which to a large extent set the pattern for later relationships, was disrupted by their betrayal of us. We were drawn into something that not only hurt us physically, emotionally or spiritually, it also had to be kept hidden, and it isolated us from other people. It meant that some of the fundamental building blocks upon which we based our view of ourselves and the world were unsafe and unstable. For this reason, much of what we came to believe about ourselves and the world around us, whatever things may have looked like from the outside, was inherently flawed. This in turn means that the relationships we formed both inside and outside our family were affected and distorted to a greater or lesser degree by those flawed beliefs.

If we were abused by people outside our immediate family, that too would have undermined our trust in relationships. Even if our family relationships were healthy, the abuse we experienced from other trusted adults will have raised in our unconscious minds the possibility that grown-ups might not be as safe and trustworthy as we had believed. In addition to this, the chances are that we were forced to keep secrets about what was happening to us from our caregivers, leading to a sense of shame that may have infected many subsequent relationships.

Attachment styles

Many of us who were abused as children have developed a pattern of *insecure attachments*. These patterns are like the foundations on which we build all the other relationships in our lives. There are lots of reasons why we might have developed insecure attachments, not all of them related to abuse. Any disruption in caregiving relationships, even if they are accidental or incidental – in other words, no one deliberately set out to cause harm – can result in children forming insecure or ambivalent attachments. This is particularly true if those disruptions happened in the first three or four years of life. However, if we were also abused, those patterns of insecure attachments take root more deeply, and can have a profound effect on how we form and maintain relationships.[21]

These difficulties with relationships are all rooted in anxiety and fear. We tend to find ourselves very anxious when it comes to forming and maintaining relationships. This goes for all of our relationships – work, social, close friendships and intimate relationships. Our anxiety is because deep down we find it hard to believe that people will want to connect with us. If they do connect with us, we are by no means certain that they can be trusted to remain connected with us. There can be lots of reasons for our anxiety, many of which are directly or indirectly related to the abuse that we have suffered.

The thing about anxiety is that if we don't find a way to manage it or push it away, it can become intolerable to us. We find ourselves driven into all sorts of strategies to avoid or escape the awful uncertainty – in the case of anxiety around relationships, the uncertainty about whether we are loved, liked or considered worthy of inclusion. The way we are in relating with people can often cause us to feel a great deal of shame. I know that for me personally one of the things that always haunts me the most is what I see as my relational failures, and in particular the fact that if I look back over my life, I can see that I have made the same mistakes over and over again. It is easy, when faced with these apparent failures, to beat ourselves up: *Why don't I ever seem to learn?*

---

[21] John Bowlby, *Attachment and Loss, Volume 1: Attachment* (London: Penguin Books, 1971).

If we are going to break free of that sense of shame, which after all is another injury that our abusers have perpetrated on us, we need to re-frame and think about these things in a different way. It is totally understandable that we form insecure attachments and therefore struggle in relationships. In effect, even with our healthy connections we are often filtering things through the patterns set by our abusive relationships. If we can look at ourselves with a little compassion and kindness, we can reduce the shame that compounds our difficulties.

It is generally reckoned that there are three different ways in which we might habitually respond to our patterns of insecure attachments.

Dismissive attachment

The truth is, if we dared to admit it, that we all need and want connection with others. But for those of us who develop an avoidant or dismissive response to our anxiety over relationships, we probably don't admit that, sometimes not even to ourselves. It doesn't necessarily mean we are shy or socially inept, though our social skills may not be as highly developed as those of other people. We can be good company and very engaging when we want to be. We could even be the life and soul of any party we go to. However, when relationships begin to develop any level of depth or complexity, we find ourselves unable to navigate that with any degree of comfort. Closer, deeper or more complex relationships involve risk. We have to invest ourselves in them. We have to acknowledge our own needs in them, and that leaves us vulnerable. Perhaps we will express needs that others are unable or unwilling to meet. Perhaps they don't really want to be our friends or have any other sort of relationship with us. Perhaps they may be like those who abused us – all pleasant and kind on the surface, but underneath they prove to be dangerous. Perhaps they only want to be close to us for what they can get out of us, or what we can do for them.

It feels vulnerable and it feels out of control, and that won't do. We need to be in control in our friendships and relationships, because that is the only way we can feel safe. Even more crucially we need to be in control of our own emotional needs, because if we let our feelings come to the surface, they will inevitably draw us into these dangerous, out-of-control relationships.

Those of us who develop a dismissive attachment style tend to respond to our anxiety by putting up both internal and external barriers. We feel a lot more comfortable when there is a considerable emotional and sometimes physical distance between ourselves and other people. We tend to minimise our need for human connection, warmth and intimacy. Sometimes we do this by placing a high value on our independence; at other times we just behave in rather stand-offish and socially exclusive ways. Either way, the net effect is that we tend to remain isolated from others, and the relationships we do have are somewhat emotionally shallow. We also tend to disconnect from our own emotions whenever we have to deal with challenging social or more intimate relational interactions.

Our whole style of relating, or perhaps of not relating, is rooted in the belief that emotional detachment from ourselves and others is the best way to keep ourselves safe and free from anxiety. The more distance we have the better. The more we deny our messy emotional responses to life and the trauma we experienced the better. Better still is if we can turn our disconnection and detachment into a virtue. There are whole cultures built around these ideas – that detachment from distressing emotions is a good thing, and that connection with others should be formalised rather than spontaneous. The traditional British stiff upper lip would be one example. The stereotypically male imperative to contain emotions within an impassive shell might be another.

The reality is that we may adopt the dismissive attachment style because superficially at least it is quite successful. It helps us to remain in control in the face of what might otherwise be distressing emotional and relational storms. However, there is a price to pay. The strategy is successful, but in a way it is *too* successful. The likelihood is that few people will see through our attachment style and understand that deep down we also have emotional and relational needs. Those needs, therefore, will most likely remain unmet, and the lack of deep emotional connection, while it may keep us 'safe' in one sense, also cuts us off from much of what we need to grow, heal and recover from the wounds caused by the abuse we experienced.

Preoccupied attachment

The preoccupied attachment style does exactly what it says on the tin. When our anxiety over the security of our relationships becomes too great, it gnaws at us, and begins to consume our thinking. We literally become *preoccupied* with how to keep hold of the relationships that we need in order to feel safe and secure.

This anxiety is a powerful force. It is rooted in the earliest days of our infancy when our mother, or whoever was the primary caregiver, was absent from us. She was our main source of food, nurture, comfort, love, etc. We could even say she was our main source of life. Without her there to feed us and keep us warm and safe, we feared that we might die or cease to exist. What if she didn't come back? What if she decided to abandon us? In the face of such overwhelming anxiety, we were driven to find ways to prevent our caregivers from leaving us. That was a very real fear when we were babies, and in some ways the response, to become preoccupied with whether our main caregiver was close enough and connected enough with us, was very rational.

When we were abused in childhood, our anxiety about the security of our connection with caregivers became magnified. The terrible and terrifying things that were happening to us made us wonder if there was something wrong with us. These things wouldn't happen to a good child, so it must mean that we are bad. If those who abused us were also our caregivers, the situation was even more scary. Surely Mummy or Daddy wouldn't do such things unless we were really, really bad. Somehow we have to win them over, to please them and placate them, not only so they don't hurt us more, but in order to prevent them abandoning us altogether.

The abuse we experienced only served to enhance the level of anxiety we felt around attachment and relationships. The fact that what we came to believe about ourselves and those who abused us wasn't true changed nothing. Most of our beliefs are not rooted in the rational part of our brains, but in the emotional, feeling parts.

For most children, those early fears of abandonment were tempered and mitigated by experience. Mostly our caregivers weren't away for long. They came back, and carried on loving and nurturing where they left off. Those children learned that it was OK if they were left for a little while, that it didn't mean they were bad or wrong. They learned to be resilient to the anxiety caused by separation.

For us as survivors, however, the story was different. We never learned that it was OK to be left on our own or to be separated from our caregivers. Either bad things happened to us when we were away from them, or they themselves did bad things to us. Either way we were consumed with shame about what had happened. It confirmed to us that we were unlovable and that no one who knew our secrets would want to be with us or stay with us.

What was a reasonable response for us when we were little became a less helpful set of responses once we were grown up. We still relate with others from that place of fear of abandonment, and of being preoccupied with doing whatever we can to avoid what feels to us like a life-threatening disaster. In practice this means that very often we are incredibly intense in relationships. We have a great internal drive to keep checking that they are really OK with us. We need constant reassurance that they really care, really like us, really love us and so on. We know, or if we don't know we are soon told, that the constant checking and seeking of verbal reassurance is not acceptable to most people, so we have to develop some more subtle strategies to reassure ourselves that we are loved and are not about to be abandoned.

As a result, we can become very clingy or needy. We try to make ourselves indispensable to our friends and loved ones, while at the same time trying anything we can to get our own needs for love, security and reassurance met.

Perhaps unsurprisingly, our neediness and dependence can become a significant issue in relationships with friends and loved ones. Often we may find ourselves entering into co-dependent relationships with people who are themselves needy in some ways. Sometimes this can feel safer for us, because if they are needy and need us, our anxiety around abandonment can be somewhat eased, at least temporarily.

The problem is that sooner or later most people will get fed up with our neediness. Even if they are needy themselves, the moment our needs begin to take centre stage on a regular basis, they will realise they cannot adequately get their emotional and nurturing needs met by us, and they will in all likelihood do the very thing that we have feared the most. They will begin to pull away from us, and may in the end abandon us altogether. Of course, this in turn only reinforces our already false and self-destructive beliefs about ourselves. We take it as confirmation of what we have always suspected: that we are bad people who are unworthy of love and belonging.

This poses a huge dilemma for us as survivors. Our healing and recovery depend on us receiving the things we didn't have in the right ways when we were growing up. This includes love, care, affirmation and nurture. However, our strategies for trying to get those things, or perhaps to avoid the risk of losing them, may be the very thing about us that drives people away. Somehow, we need to find a way to get what we need without playing out the toxic scripts of our preoccupied attachment style. We need new ways of dealing with our anxiety.

Disorganised attachment

Sometimes our anxiety feels so overwhelming, we cannot even settle on a single strategy to help us manage it. We find ourselves flipping back and forth between the other attachment styles. Some of the time we find ourselves wanting to avoid any in-depth connection either with others or with ourselves – in other words, we use the dismissive attachment style. But this in itself causes us too much anxiety. Our dismissive and avoidant responses are in danger of isolating us too much, when our need for connection is so great. In order to deal with that anxiety, we flip over into the preoccupied attachment style, desperately seeking out and clinging to the people we hope may give us the security, love and connection that we need. The problem with this is that it raises to an even greater pitch our fear of abandonment. If we allow ourselves to make those connections and engage with how emotionally needy we actually are, then the pain of separation and loss when someone finally abandons us will be all the greater. What can we do, except flip back to the other strategy, and become dismissive and avoidant again?

The problem we find as we follow this disorganised attachment strategy is that the more we flip from one to the other, the more chaotic we appear to others, and the more chaotic we may feel to ourselves. Sometimes just our inability to find a strategy that works for us, despite all our attempts, can lead to our emotions becoming very volatile. We may find ourselves experiencing mood swings, becoming angry or feeling low in response to very small things. Typically, our friendships and other relationships tend to be somewhat unstable, and we find ourselves struggling to maintain the relationships we do have, as people decide not to put up with our emotional instability.

Those of us who experience a high level of dissociation in response to trauma may well find that we default to this disorganised attachment style. The greater the degree of dissociation, the greater the likelihood that the different parts of our identity will adopt not only different attachment styles, but possibly different ways of manifesting those attachment styles. As those dissociated parts tussle for control of our consciousness, we may well find our different attachment styles coming to the fore.

Again, we have to find other ways to deal with our anxiety, and to regulate our emotions. At the same time, like all survivors of abuse and those with insecure attachments, we need to deal with the root causes of our insecure attachments and find healthy and appropriate ways of getting some of the love, care and nurture we did not receive as we were growing up.

Healing connections

In some ways the very things that we as survivors find difficult about relating with others contain within them the seeds of healing. We find ourselves challenged in so many areas when trying to navigate friendships, not to mention more intimate relationships. It can be really tempting to give up and isolate ourselves entirely (dismissive attachment style), to get drawn into co-dependent relationships with other needy and dependent people (preoccupied attachment style), or to enter into chaotic relationships with people who like ourselves have never been able to settle on a social or relational strategy. If, however, we can begin to identify some genuinely helpful and supportive relationships in our lives, and build new strategies around these, the possibility exists that they can become sources of nurture and healing for us.

Of course, this is a lot easier said than done. Allowing these genuine and authentic relationships to begin to shape our ways of responding, without either running away or clinging on to such a degree that they eventually run away, is not something we may ever really have experienced. Often the first people who have ever really tried to relate with us in consistently loving and authentic ways are our therapists and other supporters. Particularly if we were abused early in childhood, or there were other complicating factors to the trauma we experienced, we will have no appropriate grid for understanding just what these authentic, healing relationships are all about, or what the other people want from us.

We spin ourselves stories – narratives that fit the pattern we are already familiar with from previous experience. These narratives can be positive or negative. All of our fears and fantasies are played out on those who are helping and supporting us. As someone who is both a survivor and a therapist specialising in working with survivors, I am only too well aware of the intensity of the feelings that can be generated when we as survivors try to fit our new experiences of relationships into familiar and often toxic old patterns. We begin to cast our therapists and other supporters into the roles we are familiar with from our experience, or alternatively the roles we believe will best meet the needs that were not appropriately met as we were growing up.

Our positive fantasies try to create good mothers and fathers, or idealised lovers, out of those who are helping and supporting us. They are our saviours. We idealise them and absolutely refuse to entertain the possibility that they could ever make a mistake, do anything wrong or be anything less than perfect in whatever ways we need them to be. At the same time our fears try to protect us from harm by finding 'evidence' that they are actually bad, dangerous and abusive fathers, mothers or lovers, just as we are used to. We are wary and mistrustful of them, and willing to pounce on the slightest sign of weakness, tiredness, lack of insight or fallibility as evidence that they hate us or are out to do us harm.

Most often we cycle between these contradictory perspectives, sometimes within a space of days or even hours. Which way we flip is often not based on any rational logic. Though it should be said that often the ways in which we perceive those who are helping and supporting us does have its own somewhat distorted type of logic.

I once worked with a survivor who used to set me 'tests' to see if I was really going to be consistent and loving towards her. One summer I was going to be away on a four-week trip to another country. About half the trip was for a holiday, and in the other half I had some work commitments. Because it was a long break, I knew that for this young woman in particular, it could be challenging. I offered to have a Skype call with her during the work-related part of my trip. We agreed that I would email her when I had a good internet connection and we would then set up a time for our call. When I did email, having been away at that point for about ten days, she emailed back to say that she was doing well and didn't need to have a Skype call. I replied saying, 'OK, if you're sure. Let me know if you change your mind.' I didn't hear back, and thought no more about it.

When I returned from my trip and met up with her, it was clear that she was furious with me. She refused to speak to me or respond in any way at first, and when I pressed her she responded only in monosyllables. This went on for weeks, until eventually I'd had enough, and suggested that if she wasn't prepared to talk to me at least to tell me why she was so angry with me, there was little point in me continuing to work with her. Finally, she told me that I had failed her test and proved what she had always suspected, that I didn't really care for her at all. Apparently, when she had emailed to say she was doing alright and didn't need a Skype call, I was supposed to insist that we talk, which would have proved that I was really there for her.

To her, this reasoning was totally logical and reasonable. I was supposed to be able to see beyond what she said to what she actually needed. In short, I was supposed to be able to read her mind and respond appropriately. In fact, she was convinced that I had read her mind, and did know her real needs, and had simply decided on a whim not to meet those needs or to respond appropriately. Once she was able to articulate this, we were able to work through the whole issue, and were able to restore our therapeutic relationship. Indeed, our relationship became even stronger and more helpful to her as a result of us having managed to overcome this obstacle. What she fed back later was that instead of being angry with her and punishing her, I simply remained consistent and loving and real with her, at the same time as helping her to see the self-defeating nature of the script she was playing out.

For us as survivors, this is one of the key things we need to get hold of on our journey of recovery and healing. Everything about our experience of trauma makes us either want to run away from the things that feel dangerous to us or want to cling to them in unhelpful ways. However, if we can do neither of those things, but instead find ways to work them through with safe people, it opens up the possibility that we might experience something different and healing. It is that experiencing something different, assuming it is appropriate and consistent, that opens up the opportunity for us to begin to rewrite our habitual and self-defeating narratives around relationships. This in turn means that we may also be able to rewrite some of the habitual and self-defeating narratives about ourselves and what we can expect from the world.

Good enough helpers

Everything we have talked about so far in this chapter could make it sound as if we need our therapists and supporters to be perfect people. However, this is in fact not the case. We might *like* them to be perfect. We might like them to never make a mistake, never have an off day, never say or do the wrong thing. But in the long run this would not be helpful. It is all part of our idealistic fantasy that if we can only have perfect relationships with perfect people, then we can be fixed and never have to worry about anything ever again.

The problem of course is that there are no perfect people this side of heaven. Therapists and other people in helping roles are all too fallible. They have days when they're not as sharp as other days. Days when they get out of bed the wrong side and lack their usual gracious patience with us. There are days when they may say or do the 'wrong' thing, and inadvertently offend, trigger or upset us in some way. Nor are there any other perfect relationships.

I have to be honest and say that as a therapist as well as a survivor, I find the thought of having to be perfect or infallible to be pretty intimidating, and yet, there are plenty of occasions when, drawn in by the needs of a survivor, I have tried to fulfil the role of perfect, all-wise, all-knowing, all-powerful therapist. I have come to realise that it is usually on these occasions that I make my biggest mistakes. When I am able to embrace the idea that it is OK for me not to be perfect or infallible, I feel a great sense of relief. I am able to relax and be who I really am. Unsurprisingly, these are the times, when I am at my most authentic, that I and the survivors I am working with see the greatest progress. I do not have to be perfect. I only need to be *good enough*.

The truth is that what we as survivors need in our helpers is not perfection. What we need is for them to be good enough for us. This concept of *good enough* was something I first came across when I worked in Social

265

Services with children and their families. Often people believe they are failing as parents because they are not perfect. Sometimes when we feel we are failing, we stop trying, because there seems no point putting in the effort if what we are aiming for feels unachievable. Good enough parenting is not perfect. A good enough parent makes mistakes. But what they also do is to take responsibility for their mistakes, and do their best to put them right. For those of us who were abused and maltreated within our immediate family, it was not the result of having imperfect parents. Rather, it was the result of having parents who were not good enough. Even for those of us who were abused outside our immediate family, our parents and caregivers may not have been good enough – especially if they failed to protect us, disbelieved us, or made us feel that the abuse was our fault.

What we need from our therapists, and from our pastors and other supporters, is not perfection. If we seem to demand it, it is because we are afraid that our helpers may fall short or prove to be just like all of those who abused or failed us in other ways. However, that is a demand that inevitably will not and cannot be met. This is as it should be. As survivors we have to learn to navigate our way through all these imperfect relationships as part of our recovery. The relationships we have with our therapists and other helpers, along with all the ups and downs, provide an excellent model. They will undoubtedly make mistakes with us. They will say the wrong thing or do the wrong thing, but if they are good enough for us they will take responsibility for their mistakes, apologise and do whatever needs doing to put it right.

Them being good enough, but not perfect, will also help us to learn how to be good enough for others. We too will make mistakes. We too will get things wrong. We will not be the perfect client, colleague or friend. Because of the pain and distress that gets triggered in us, not to mention our own insecure attachment styles, there are going to be times when, to be frank, we will probably be quite hard work. We may even act in some fairly offensive ways, and say horrible things to those trying to help us – not because we want to, but as a result of all the chaotic feelings we are carrying. Having to navigate our own reactions with people who can be trusted not to punish, reject or abandon us because we have got things wrong, is priceless to us in terms of our journey of recovery and healing.

Let's talk about sex

For survivors of abuse, and particularly for those of us who have survived sexual abuse as children, there can be few topics as complex or as fraught as that of sex, sexual relationships and indeed sexuality. The things that happened to us as children took place when our sexual identity and sexual responses were still in the process of being formed. We were made to take part in, or exposed to, activity that we did not have the emotional, mental or physical capacity to understand. What happened took place without our informed consent. We were powerless and bewildered as we were overwhelmed by a flood of physical sensations and emotions that we did not yet have fully developed concepts for. At the same time, we lived and continue to live in a world that bombards us with mixed messages about sex and sexuality. On the one hand, sexual experience is something to be desired, craved and even obsessed over. It gives us status, it makes us cool, it is a sign that we are grown up and sophisticated. We are surrounded by sexualised images of women and men in entertainment, sport and advertising. On the other hand, sex is something dirty, shameful and not to be talked about. At best it is a subject of questionable humour, something to be laughed about with trusted friends, but hidden from those who might not approve. Sexual images and material that are not considered 'art' are considered to be pornographic.

To compound the problem, the Church has historically not dealt well with issues around sex and sexuality. This is largely because the Church takes seriously its role in giving a moral lead, which is a very good and needed thing. The problem comes when a particular church and its leaders haven't fully embraced the real good news. It tends to focus on external behaviour, rather than understanding the root causes of that behaviour. As a result, many people find themselves met with criticism and condemnation rather than understanding and encouragement.

These contradictions can cause considerable confusion and distress even among the general population, who presumably had what passes for a normal upbringing in terms of sex and sexuality. How much greater, then, is the confusion and distress experienced by survivors of sexual abuse and exploitation, for whom nothing about sex and sexuality was ever normal or healthy.

In one sense this entire chapter could consist of answers to variations on the question, 'Is it normal for me to think/feel/do…?'

In truth, there is no one single, normal set of reactions we ought to have regarding issues around sex and sexuality. Our responses as survivors can go in many different directions. If we think about survivors as a whole, we are likely to experience the whole range of human sexual behaviour and orientation. The one thing we probably can say is common to all of us as survivors of sexual abuse is that our experience of sex and sexuality as adults is likely to be complex and not straightforward.

The most honest general response to the 'Is it normal...' question is: 'Yes, it is a totally normal response to childhood experiences that were very abnormal.' However, given all of society's confusion around sex and sexuality, not to mention our own complex reactions to what happened to us, no general response is likely to be sufficient. Our sense of shame and confusion over what happened to us is almost certainly so great that,? whether consciously or unconsciously, most of us are going to be convinced that what we are feeling, thinking, doing or not doing in terms of sexuality is probably way outside the bounds both of normality and acceptability.

Sexual orientation

We live in a world where public attitudes to sexual orientation and lifestyles other than strictly monogamous heterosexuality are changing and developing all the time. In my own lifetime, the way that we see things such as homosexuality has changed out of all recognition. When I was a small child, sexual activity between people of the same gender was illegal and punishable by time in prison. As I grew up, it became legal, with some restrictions, but was still considered unacceptable and perverted by mainstream society. Gradually attitudes have shifted, and the legal restrictions have been removed (at least in most parts of the UK). Gay people can now legally get married, and while they may still face prejudice and discrimination in some quarters, at least officially and to a large extent socially, homosexuality is now considered both acceptable and normal.

However, this does not mean that all the difficult and complex feelings around sexual orientation have gone away, especially for survivors of sexual abuse. In particular, one of the questions survivors often ask themselves is, 'Am I gay/bisexual/asexual/transgender because I was abused?'

It would be nice if we had a simple and straightforward answer to this, but the truth is there is no such thing. There are numerous theories about why people settle into a particular sexual orientation. Many believe it is a matter of genetics – that some people are simply born gay. Others believe that it has to do with early family dynamics – that people learn to be gay, but so early on that it isn't something they have any choice about. Others, including many in the Church, believe that being gay is a lifestyle choice and that it is 'sinful' or 'unnatural'. The truth is that for all the claims made to the contrary, nobody really knows. What we do know is that somewhere between 5 and 10 per cent of the population will fairly consistently identify themselves as gay, and that many of them report that they have felt this way for as long as they can remember. We also know that there is a section of the population, perhaps around 20 to 30 per cent, who experience their sexual orientation as somewhat more fluid, and at least 60 per cent of the population have had at least one sexual encounter with someone of the same gender.[22]

My personal view is that sexual orientation is probably influenced by a number of factors. Some of it may be genetic, some of it may be family dynamics and some of it may be other factors. However, at this point I don't believe it is possible to say exactly what the balance of those factors is. In some ways it would seem strange if the sexual abuse we experienced did not have at least some impact on our sexual orientation. But the truth is there is little or no way of knowing how much influence that had or in what ways we were influenced.

My own experience was of being abused mostly by men, but also by a few women. During my late teenage years, I would probably have identified myself as primarily gay, with occasional explorations into straight territory. Certainly, the social circles I moved in were supportive of such a self-identification. As I grew older my orientation gradually shifted. By my mid-twenties I had lost interest in sexual activity with other men, and became more interested in sexual activity with women. It wasn't something I tried to do, or did because I was particularly unhappy with my previous identification. It was just something that happened. I am reasonably convinced, without being able to prove it or demonstrate how, that my earlier identification as gay may well have been connected to the fact that I was subjected to sexual abuse and exploitation by many men from preschool age up until I

---

[22] June M Reinisch, *The Kinsey Institute New Report on Sex* (New York: St Martin's Press, 1991).

was in my late teens. This was the form of sexuality that was 'normal' in my experience. That, coupled with the hormonal surges of puberty and adolescence, which can so easily cause us to latch on to sexual experiences and take them as a pattern for future activity, made the self-identification as gay seem natural at the time, even though it did not endure in the long run.

On the other hand, I know of others who, having had similar experiences of sexual abuse by men, respond by becoming aggressively heterosexual in their behaviour, and developing views that are quite homophobic in nature.

The point seems to be that the sexual abuse we experience when young causes us to derive meaning from later feelings and experiences, and the patterns of meaning that we discover and make for ourselves contribute at least in part to the ways in which we define our sexual orientation. However, it is not possible to predict the ways in which we will respond, or indeed how our responses may change over time. What we can recognise is our need for self-compassion. We are likely to have strong feelings about our sexual orientation – either positive or negative, or indeed simply confused. Self-compassion and an understanding of the role played by the abuse we experienced will help us to deal with those feelings in a more healthy and helpful way.

Sex triggers me

For many of us who were sexually abused as children, sexual activity, even if it is consensual or with a safe person, doesn't always feel safe. In fact, it can feel downright scary, disgusting or overwhelming. This is something that can manifest for us in a number of ways.

Sometimes we may be aware of those feelings of fear or disgust or distress. At other times, particularly if we dissociate, our minds may protect us even from feeling those unpleasant emotions, and our response to sexual activity can manifest as a lack of interest or a loss of libido. At other times we may have a strong post-traumatic reaction and be triggered, which results in us freezing or going numb.

For some of us it is all sexual activity or even references to sexual activity that triggers us. For others of us, there may be some categories of sexual activity or references that trigger us, while others don't seem to affect us in the same way. For example, some of us may feel absolutely OK with sexual touch and play, but the moment it develops into any form of penetrative sexual activity we become seriously triggered. Some may have sexual thoughts and feelings, and may masturbate either occasionally or regularly, but find that any sexual activity involving others is impossible.

It's hardly surprising that we are triggered. The hurt child inside us may well categorise any sexual activity or even our own sexual feelings as dangerous, scary, disgusting or dirty. We may go numb and unfeeling, or we may freeze in terror and be unable to respond, or we may physically be unable to join in with sexual activity. Sometimes we avoid the kind of relationships that might lead to sexual activity altogether, and in some ways this might feel like a reasonable course of action for anyone feeling the need to protect themselves. But of course, things are rarely that simple and straightforward.

While the hurt and abused child inside us may well want to protect themselves and freeze or flee from the many potential triggers of sexual activity, as with all manifestations of freeze and flight reactions to traumatic triggers, this is only partially helpful. It is helpful because it may protect us from experiences that would be overwhelming until and unless we are ready to deal with them. On the other hand, it comes at a cost in terms of forming and maintaining intimate relationships, not to mention having to navigate a highly sexualised world.

It is absolutely vital for us as survivors of sexual abuse that we do not in any way feel pressure to conform to the expectations of others or the prevailing culture in terms of having an active sex life. The bottom line is that if it feels safer for us not to engage in any particular form of sexual activity, there is no way we should be made to feel we have to override our own boundaries in that respect. However, at the same time, it is also OK if we wish to make recovering a healthy sexuality part of our healing journey. Many of us despair of ever being able to be healed in this area of our lives, but if we are able to process and make sense of the traumatic experiences that are the root of our difficulties, we may well, with help, be able to come to a place of greater wholeness and freedom in the expression of our sexuality.

Is it wrong that I responded?

She sits opposite me with her hair hiding her face, and her shoulders hunched over. She is the very picture of shame. When she begins to speak it is in a voice so soft it is hard for me to hear clearly, and with many false starts and hesitations.

'I know it was my fault. I know I deserved what he did to me.'

She is speaking about the sexual abuse she experienced from the age of eight at the hands of one of her uncles. It is very common for survivors to blame themselves for what happened, but there are usually specific reasons why this might be so. I wonder aloud what might be causing her to think in this way. If anything, the body language of shame becomes even more intense, and there is a long silence of over a minute. Finally she begins to speak again.

'I liked it... I mean, it was horrible and scary... but it sort of made me feel nice... you know... down there.'

She risks a quick glance up to see how I'm reacting before continuing.

'I know that makes me disgusting. An evil person. I don't deserve anyone's sympathy.'

One of the most difficult and distressing things for survivors of sexual abuse to come to terms with is exactly this very common reaction. Sexual abuse makes us feel horrible. We feel frightened, degraded, ashamed and dirty. Sometimes it is also a physically painful experience. However, at the same time, many of us find that we have a purely physical response to the sexual stimulation. It is awful, but some part of us feels a pleasurable response. The result can be even greater shame.

There are also times when, because we are able to dissociate, we split off a part of us that seems able to try to deal with the abuse. Sometimes that part of us appears to cooperate with the abusers. That part may even believe that they are a willing party to what is happening. This too, when we look back on it at a later date, can cause us to feel even more shame.

There are a few things we need to remember to help us get free of the shame.

The first is to remember that what we felt was a purely physiological response. It was involuntary and therefore it was not under our control. We don't need to feel responsible or to blame for the fact that our body responded with pleasure, any more than we need to feel responsible for the times that our body responded to things with pain or discomfort.

The second thing to remember is that the fact that our bodies responded with pleasure does not in any way or under any circumstances make what our abusers did to us OK. What they did was wrong by any standard. There is never any excuse for sexual abuse or exploitation. As children we were not able to give informed consent to what they did, or what they wanted us to do. Responding in this way does not imply consent in any way, shape or form. Neither does an involuntary pleasure response mean we enjoyed what was being done to us.

A third thing to remember is that even though we may have dissociated, and a part of us may have appeared to enjoy and cooperate with the abuse, the reality is somewhat different. The fact that we dissociated is in itself evidence that we experienced what was happening to us as frightening and threatening. We dissociated because the strategy of submitting and pleasing our abusers seemed like the best way to help us to stay as safe as possible. At the time when it was happening, we didn't believe we had an alternative. There was no real safe way of refusing our consent, and in all likelihood there was no one in our lives, no safe grown-up, we could turn to for help.

For those of us who feel the shame of having responded to our abusers, there is as always a journey to walk before we can feel fully free of it. But we are not alone. God does not see any shame on us. Even through our brokenness He sees us as beautiful and perfect.[23] Those who are helping and supporting us, if they are truly the body of Christ for us, will stay with us and love us along the way.

I'm fixated on aspects of the abuse

Sometimes, when we have been sexually abused, we may find that our minds fixate on some aspects of the abuse. The sexual acts that we were made to participate in can invade our fantasy life, so that we think about it some or all of the time in connection with feeling sexually aroused. It is actually very common for survivors to find themselves wanting to repeat compulsively some of the things that happened to them. Sometimes we may act out some elements of the abuse – playing sexual games with partners that involve us being forced, or re-enacting some other aspect of the abuse. Sometimes survivors masturbate while fantasising about some aspect of the abuse being re-enacted. At other times the compulsion to re-enact manifests in a more subtle way. For example, by our picking partners who are themselves abusive in similar ways to those who originally abused us, or perhaps by placing ourselves in risky or even dangerous situations.

---

[23] God sees both the beauty and perfection of our true selves, and the brokenness and dislocation of our false selves. For many survivors the damage to their identity is so great, they need to know that in God's eyes they are beautiful and lovable as they are, before they can reciprocate and receive His unconditional love in their lives through Christ.

All of these things can greatly contribute to the shame we feel about our sexuality and its connection to the abuse we experienced. However, again we need to understand what is actually going on for us, and allow that to guide our self-compassion. Sometimes when we were growing up our minds tried to lessen the impact of what was being done to us by trying to normalise it. When we become fixated on aspects of the abuse in any of these ways, it is as if our unconscious mind is still trying to normalise the whole area of sex and sexuality for us. That may seem a little odd or misguided, but it is as if by repeating what happened to us in a less dangerous and more controllable form, some part of us is trying to make things better.

The reality is that all of these difficulties that survivors commonly have with sex and sexuality are not simple to resolve. We can begin to work on the shame that we feel about them, but these are complex issues. In order to navigate the minefield resulting not just from the abuse we experienced, but also from the fractured way in which society, culture and the Church view sex and sexuality, we will probably need the skilled help of a therapist.

Supporter's Pause for Thought: Being good enough

If you are one of our friends and supporters, you may be worrying right now that there is pressure on you to be perfect – that we expect you always to be caring and always present for us. The truth is that you don't have to be perfect at all. In all honesty, though, that can get complicated a bit by the fact that as survivors we do sometimes act as if we expect those helping and supporting us always to get it right. That isn't a reflection on you. It is about our fear that you, like so many others, might turn out to be abusive or in other ways not helpful to us.

In reality we know that you cannot be perfect. We know that you will make mistakes. This may be hard for us to navigate sometimes, particularly when we are triggered and scared. But a large part of what makes you different for us is that you don't try to pretend that you always get it right. Our abusers were never wrong in their own eyes. Often they made everything our fault. They rarely if ever apologised, or if they did, it was mostly self-serving and intended to manipulate us.

When you make a mistake or get something wrong for us, it is possible we could react out of our brokenness and give you a hard time. But you recognising and acknowledging your mistakes and giving us a genuine apology may well be something new for us. The fact that you continue to love and care for us, even if we are a bit harsh with you, speaks more to us than you can ever know.

Being 'good enough' for us means that your intentions towards us are good. It means that you love and care for us. It means that you are honest with us, and don't try to manipulate us or control us. It means that when you make mistakes you don't try to cover it up or make it our fault, but take responsibility and do your best to put things right. When you are 'good enough' we learn all sorts of important things from you. We learn that it is OK for us to make mistakes too, and that when we do, there are ways to put things right that don't involve us being punished. We learn that even when we may not be acting as our kindest, most patient selves, that we are still loved and lovable. We learn that we will not be rejected and abandoned by those who say they love and care for us. We learn that we have value and worth to you, and that just possibly we may not be quite as bad as we thought.

Chapter Eleven
The Trauma-informed Church

Trauma-informed

There is a phrase that has gained common currency in the world of counselling and psychotherapy in recent years: *trauma-informed*. It is used to describe professionals and services that are aware of some of the latest thinking about trauma and how best to support survivors.

Survivors need authentic community. We need safe and healthy family. We need a strong and life-giving connection with our Creator. In short, we need church. Though we may have our personal preferences, it really isn't important whether it is a liturgical church or something more informal. It isn't important whether they have modern worship music or sing hymns. It may not be important whether it is a large congregation in a public building or something that meets in a living room. What is important for survivors is that whatever it looks like, church is able to be an integral part of our journey of recovery and healing.

Church has the potential to provide much of the spiritual input that we need, and also much of the community support that we need. But if it is going to do that, it needs to become something that up until now it has struggled to be, and that is trauma-informed. This is partly about education and training, but it is also about a fundamental shift in attitudes and priorities. A trauma-informed church above all else has to become a safe space for survivors, because without safety, survivors will not stick around, let alone be able to grow and heal. Safety means a great deal more than simply keeping people physically safe. We also need emotional and spiritual safety if church is going to become all that we need it to be: a part of the solution, rather than just another part of the problem.

Many of the ways in which some churches have failed survivors are the result of ignorance and misunderstanding rather than any bad intent. If a church does not understand the nature of trauma, and in particular childhood abuse and the impact it can have on us, it will inevitably make mistakes. Now, of course, mistakes are normal. They are part of life, learning and growth. But where survivors are concerned it is important that the church quickly learns to minimise those mistakes. Survivors are strong and resilient, but we are also fragile and broken. Church and its leaders are authoritative voices in our world. This is potentially a hugely positive thing, but with that authority comes power, and with that power comes the responsibility to use it wisely – not just for the benefit of all, but in particular for the benefit of the most broken and powerless. When the church and church leaders make mistakes when dealing with survivors, it can greatly compound a lot of the damage caused by the abuse we experienced.

For that reason, there are a number of things that a church needs to have in place to make it a safe space for survivors – one in which they can grow, recover and heal, rather than one in which they will feel restricted, excluded or controlled.

This is perhaps part of what Jesus is hoping we will grasp.

> Are you tired? Worn out? Burned out on religion? Come to me. Get away with me and you'll recover your life. I'll show you how to take a real rest. Walk with me and work with me – watch how I do it. Learn the unforced rhythms of grace. I won't lay anything heavy or ill-fitting on you. Keep company with me and you'll learn to live freely and lightly.
> *Matthew 11:28-30* (The Message)

Safeguarding

Every trauma-informed church needs to have in place comprehensive policies and procedures. By this we mean more than just the usual child protection policy, though of course that is important. We mean a range of policies and procedures that define how the church is going to respond to vulnerable people, whether they are children or adults. The reality is that survivors by definition are vulnerable. They are vulnerable to being triggered. They are vulnerable to being shamed, exploited, controlled and manipulated. That doesn't take anything away from their strength and resilience. It doesn't mean they won't grow beyond those vulnerabilities. It simply means that for many of us we still struggle with life from time to time.

How is the church going to respond when we are triggered? How is it going to respond when we don't necessarily behave in the ways that might be expected of us? How is it going to react when our marriages come under strain because of the wounds we are carrying? How about when we come into a meeting smelling of alcohol, because it's the only way we can face dealing with that large a group of people without having a panic attack? What is your first step when a survivor feels that someone in authority in the church has done or said something inappropriate? What are your next steps after the first one? What are you going to do when you can't get someone calmed down, and you're worried they might harm themselves or try to end their life?

All of these are real scenarios that can easily happen in a church that welcomes survivors. Without a safeguarding *plan* in place, the chances are that the church will default to its traditional positions, based on lack of information and misunderstanding. A plan is more than policies and procedures; it is what results when some of these things are thought about and people really consider what the most helpful and responses to some of these situations might be.

It's also worth asking what we mean by 'the church'? Does it mean the clergy or ministers? Does it mean the wider leadership – those leading small groups and ministries within the church? Does it perhaps mean every member of the body? It is all very well for the leaders to respond to survivors in crisis in a helpful way, but all of that can be undone by some well-intentioned but ill-informed members of the congregation doing and saying things that cut across what the leaders are trying to do. To become a really safe space for survivors, the safeguarding plan needs to involve everyone. It also needs to be flexible, to adapt to changing needs over time, which means there has to be some mechanism for consultation, feedback and review.

If you are a church leader, this might sound a little daunting, but it really isn't rocket science. These are the sorts of things that all churches should at least be thinking about, even if with smaller congregations the elements of any plan are less formalised. Perhaps a good starting point is to identify some survivors who would be willing to sit down with the leadership of your church and share about their experiences, and what they think they may need to help them feel safer.

Working alongside professionals

A trauma-informed church needs to be willing to work alongside mental health professionals, such as counsellors and psychotherapists, when it comes to supporting survivors of abuse. Prayer and other spiritual input are important. Supportive community is important. But the chances are that for much of the journey of recovery and healing, the input of therapists and others with experience and skill in helping survivors is probably going to be needed. This means among other things that it is not OK for churches to treat mental health professionals as agents of the enemy. Rather, try to see them as a resource with experience and skills that can greatly help the church in supporting survivors. There are some specific outworkings of this that need to be embraced, first by the leadership, but also by everyone in the church. For example, no one in church should ever discourage a survivor from seeking proper therapeutic support. No one in church should ever tell a survivor that they should simply stop taking any psychiatric medication. Where changes need to be made in the support or input that a survivor is receiving, this should always be done in consultation with survivors and their therapists and other supporters, not coerced by super-spiritualised guilt-tripping.

It is also important to realise what *working alongside* actually means in practice. It does not mean simply referring survivors on to the professionals and then either washing your hands of them or carrying on as usual. It means talking with the therapists and others to find out what it is that the church can provide that is going to be most helpful to those on their journey of recovery and healing. It means being willing to adapt some of what you do, for example some of how you pray for people, on the advice of those whose job it is to understand the impact this might have on survivors.

To be fair, this is also something of a two-way street. Mental health professionals haven't always been the best at working alongside churches for the benefit of survivors. All too often the professionals display a degree of arrogance in thinking that they and only they have the answers for survivors. It is also true that not all mental health professionals are themselves trauma-informed, or have the resources available to respond appropriately. One important role a trauma-informed church can play is to advocate on behalf of survivors, and help them to identify and access the most appropriate forms of professional input.

Education and training

Proper education and training are vital if a church is going to become trauma-informed and learn to support survivors of abuse more effectively. This doesn't mean that every church has to have trained counsellors and therapists in its congregation. It simply means that those in leadership, in particular, and the rest of the church in general need to have a basic level of understanding. It isn't OK for those who follow Jesus to remain ignorant of those in need. Otherwise church becomes just another bunch of religious people, no different from the priest and the Levite in the parable of the Good Samaritan (Luke 10:25-37).

Survivors of abuse are all too often left metaphorically naked and bleeding by the side of the Jericho road. Those who love and follow Jesus have the resources to help them at least to some degree. But first they have to be willing to see what is in front of their eyes. They also have to be willing to do whatever they can, even if it isn't everything that is needed. In the parable, the Samaritan noticed and administered first aid, before taking the wounded person to a place where he could get more help. We aren't expecting you to work miracles for us. We know our wounds look ugly and can even be frightening to those who aren't used to dealing with such things. Just noticing and responding with ordinary kindness is a good start. But we also need you to inform yourselves, and not hide behind your ignorance. With education about what to look out for, and training in how to provide basic help and support, the church can do a great deal to alleviate our suffering. It can also help to point us in the direction of people and places where we can get more specialised help.

There is also a need for some in the church to be trained to a slightly deeper level. General emotional first aid is always going to be helpful, but there will be times when survivors are going to need a greater level of support. Those who are serving the church in pastoral care, prayer ministry or inner-healing ministry definitely need to have a greater level of understanding about trauma and abuse, and how to provide effective support to survivors.

There is plenty of general training around to inform people about abuse, and how to support survivors. Some courses are quite specialised, and aimed at professionals. However, there are others that are more aimed at helping to inform and educate family, friends and other supporters of survivors. There are even specific Christian training courses tailored to the needs of churches, ministries and other believers. I founded a charity that was partly set up to provide this sort of training and education to the Christian community. The charity is called Breakthrough, and you can find out more about what we offer at: www.traumabreakthrough.org.

Survivor support groups

When a church is trauma-informed it opens up all sorts of possibilities for supporting survivors that did not exist before. One of the things that I have always encouraged the survivors I am helping to do, is to identify a small group of people who can be called together as a support group. This can often be quite challenging for survivors, who may not always be able to identify more than one or two people to be part of this.

Perhaps one of the most important things that can help us on our journey of recovery and healing is to feel that we are not on our own. We need to have people around us who we know understand something of what we are going through. We need people we can trust. They don't have to be experts, but they do need to care. They need to be willing to take the initiative sometimes just to ask the questions to find out how we are *really* doing. They also need to be those who will respond in a crisis.

Church can be an ideal context for creating small groups of people who come together to support survivors in different ways. These groups don't have to have a large number of people in them. In fact, better that they don't. Typically, survivors may not be comfortable with too many people having input into their lives at the same time. On the other hand, they need not be too small either. The whole point about a support group is that no one should be left supporting a survivor on their own. At the same time, survivors need to know that there are a number of options to get support and help when they need it. Ideally, a support group will have between six and eight people, plus the survivor's therapist or other professional helper, and usually someone representing the church leadership.

The criteria for what makes a good support group are not complicated.

Everyone should ideally have a basic level of training about trauma and abuse.

Everyone will have some sort of positive personal connection with the survivor. The survivor also needs to trust them at least enough to be willing for them to know about some of the abuse they have experienced.

Everyone needs to be willing to give a little bit of time to supporting the survivor in different ways. It doesn't necessarily need to be very much time. It could be just a few minutes a week, but there will probably be one or two people who might be willing to give an hour or two a week on a reasonably regular basis.

Some people may be willing to be contacted by the survivor at any time in any way. Others may put boundaries around their availability.

Not everyone in the group will support in the same ways. Some may be willing to sit with a survivor while they are distressed or having a panic attack. Some may be willing to offer mostly social contact or practical support. Others may be prepared to pray in an informed way on a regular basis.

One of the main functions of a support group is to plan what to do in specific circumstances. How to respond to a call for help. How to support each other when one of them is concerned about the survivor. What to do when they feel that more help than they can provide is needed.

Everything is done in agreement with the person being supported. In fact, they are seen as an integral part of the group, not just as the passive recipient of the group's time and energy.

It is likely that the group won't actually meet together very often – perhaps regularly every six months to review how things are going and to agree any changes that need to be made. Sometimes the group might need to meet together at other times, either to respond to a particular crisis, or if something about the group is changing, such as a member leaving.

In a very real sense, this type of small group can become something of a healthy and appropriate family, and can provide a safe context for those who have been abused to find hope and healing.

Chapter Twelve
Grief and Hope

Acknowledging our loss

The journey of recovery and healing for survivors of abuse is also a journey of grief and hope.

The effect of abuse on us, both back when it was still happening and now years later, represents a huge personal loss. We have lost so many things in so many areas of our lives. As children we lost our innocence, we lost our dignity, we lost something of our joy. In a very real sense, some of us may feel that we lost our entire childhood. In the longer term, many of us have lost some very tangible things from our adult lives as well. Some of us lost our sobriety to drink and drugs. Some of us lost our health owing to the strain of living with the aftermath of severe trauma. We may have lost friendships, marriages and connections. We may even have lost our sanity, overwhelmed by the pain and distress. Some have even lost their lives because of abuse – either killed by the perpetrators, or because they simply were unable to go on living with the pain any longer.

Loss is an inevitable part of the legacy of abuse. Our entire lives are lived in its shadow until and unless we are able to face up to all that we have lost or had stolen from us. Acknowledging the loss and the pain associated with it is an essential part of the grieving process.

Grief is not simply sadness over what we have lost, nor should we see it in a negative light. Grief is how we process our loss and all the feelings associated with it. When we have lost as much as we have, we *have* to grieve. Sooner or later we have to embrace what is always a difficult and painful process in order to take us further on our journey of recovery.

There is a well-recognised process of grieving[24] that everyone goes through when dealing with loss, whether that is a bereavement or the loss associated with abuse. In truth it is probably better not to think of these things as happening in strict sequence, since some of them can happen at any time, and may well need to be repeated. However, the elements of grief are:

- Denial – this usually comes first. We don't want to believe what has happened, we don't want to engage with our sense of loss and pain, so we ignore or numb ourselves to it.

- Anger – there is a sense of outrage and unfairness about what has happened to us, and what it has cost us. We want to look around for someone or something to blame.

---

[24] Elizabeth Kübler-Ross, *On Grief and Grieving: Finding the Meaning of Grief Through the Five Stages of Loss* (London: Simon & Schuster, 2005).

- Bargaining – for survivors, this often takes the form of an unwillingness to embrace the full awfulness of what happened. We tell ourselves, 'At least x didn't happen to me,' or 'At least it wasn't y who did this to me.' We want to believe that these things make what happened to us better, or the loss less painful.

- Depression – when our bargaining strategy fails, and we realise that our rationalisations don't make what happened to us any less painful, our mood can take a nosedive. When we find that for all our outrage and anger at the unfairness of what happened, we cannot effectively displace our pain elsewhere, we may often lose motivation and become overwhelmed by sadness and depression.

- Acceptance – after we have experienced all the other elements of grief in full, we can with help come through to a place of acceptance. This does not mean that what happened to us was OK or that we stop feeling pain and distress. What it does mean is that we can, while fully feeling that pain and distress, begin to recover and grow and heal.

Unlike a simple bereavement, the grieving process associated with abuse is not likely to be a one-off thing. Usually we will need to repeat the process several times at different points during our recovery. This is because the loss we experienced as a result of the abuse is not always immediately obvious. In fact, the further we go on the journey of recovery, the more we are likely to realise we have lost. Each time we have such a realisation, we have to go through that process of grieving once again, though each time we go through it, we may recognise it and embrace it sooner.

It is usually only once we have been through this grieving process several times and come through to a place of acceptance that we can even begin to think in a realistic way about whether we wish to or are able to forgive.

Honouring our scars

All of us who were abused as children bear scars. For some of us those scars may be physical, the legacy of the injuries that were inflicted on us, or that we felt we had no choice but to inflict upon ourselves. For all of us there are emotional scars, caused by the trauma and the lack of love and care that we experienced.

Once, all of our scars were open wounds. For some of us they may still be. What the journey of recovery and healing does is to gradually clean, disinfect and bind up those emotional wounds. Over time and with the right help, the open wounds close. But there are some wounds that will always leave a scar. Many of us feel ashamed that after years of help and healing we are still showing scars on our bodies or scars on our emotions. But there is no shame in bearing scars. These are the wounds of battle. They are the honourable legacy of a huge struggle in which we have emerged victorious.

Yes, they are a reminder of the awful things that happened to us, but the reality is that we cannot and should not forget those things. They don't have to invade and blight our lives, but remembering them means we are more likely to protect and nurture ourselves and those we love and care about. On a very personal note, I know that it is my own scars that have caused me to specialise in working with survivors. It is those scars that remind me and allow me to continue to empathise with those who are still struggling with their open wounds. It is those scars that when their pain causes me to slip back into old patterns, reminds me that I am in Henri Nouwen's phrase, a *Wounded Healer*.[25]

Our scars, I believe, bring us especially close to Jesus, the original wounded healer; not only because of His well-documented love for the most broken and marginalised, but because He too still bears the scars of His greatest trial and pain. In a spiritual sense, this is part of our inheritance in Christ. Our journey of wounding and healing leaves us with scars, but our scars like His are marks of victory.

Allowing ourselves to hope

The modern Greek poet C P Cavafy, in his poem 'Ithaka', which is about both the legendary ten-year voyage home of Odysseus as he returned from the Trojan War, and about the journeys of hope and discovery that we must all make for our emotional and spiritual well-being, says this:

> Keep Ithaka always in your mind.
> Arriving there is what you're destined for.
> But don't hurry the journey at all.[26]

---

[25] Henri Nouwen, *Wounded Healer* (London: Darton, Longman & Todd, 2014).
[26] Constantine P Cavafy, *Collected Poems* (London: Chatto & Windus, 1990).

Our journey of recovery is not only one of grief. It is also one of hope. One of the most precious things we lost when we were abused was hope. We found ourselves in situations that not only damaged us, but were also inescapable. While the abuse was still happening, and perhaps at many times since, we may have felt hopeless, and as if there was no way out.

One of the things I have noticed, both about myself and about many of the survivors I work with, is that we tend towards being pessimistic. Many of us find it very hard at times to look to the future with any sort of optimism or hope. This dates back to those awful times when we had no sense as children that our abusive ordeal was ever going to end. Even if we were abused just once, while it was happening it almost certainly seemed to last much longer than it did in reality. If we were abused over a long period of time, it may for much of our lives have seemed impossible to think about or believe in an abuse-free future.

On this journey of recovery and healing we learn to hope for what we may never have had. We learn to hope that we will not always be in pain. We learn to hope that there will be days that feel better than today. We learn to hope that there may be good people in our lives. We learn to hope that one day we may deal with our triggers and panics differently. We learn to hope that the memories will intrude upon us less. We learn to hope that there are positive experiences and feelings, maybe things we don't even have a name for that will one day be ours. We learn to hope that we are more than the sum of our abusive experiences. We learn to hope that we might be unconditionally loved. We learn to hope that we might begin to like or even love ourselves.

We learn to hope, and as we hope, we learn to believe. We learn to believe in ourselves. We learn to believe that we are victorious. We learn to believe in the One who was broken, wounded and scarred, and who lost everything, even His life, before being raised to glory. We learn to believe that in Him, our journey takes us into an abundant life overflowing with goodness, joy and peace.

Poem
A Healing Journey

Let me walk with you
On this way of sorrows,
Though the journey twists
And the end,
If only you could believe in one,
Is hidden.

Let me listen to the stories
You cannot bear to tell,
That must be told,
Because left unspoken
They will turn your heart to stone
And shatter it.

Let me sit with you as you weep,
Afraid you will not stop,
Afraid you might drown,
And along with you
All you have ever loved
Be swept away.

Let me stand with you
As you face the creatures of the night
Whose too-familiar features
Haunt your sleep,
And worse,
Stay with you when you wake.

Let me hold your hand
When there are no answers,
No reasons you can hear
Or understand
But without which little warmth
You might just die of cold.

Let me walk, listen, sit,
Stand and hold;
However long the journey.
Believing when you cannot,
Hoping when you have none,
That this way of sorrows
Will one day turn to dancing.